Visual Basic 2005 Jumpstart

Other Microsoft Windows Resources from O'Reilly

Related titles
Programming Visual
  Basic 2005
Visual Basic 2005: A
  Developer's Notebook
Visual Studio Hacks

ASP.NET 2.0: A
  Developer's Notebook
Programming .NET
  Components

**Windows Books
Resource Center**
windows.oreilly.com is a complete catalog of O'Reilly's Windows and Office books, including sample chapters and code examples.

oreillynet.com is the essential portal for developers interested in open and emerging technologies, including new platforms, programming languages, and operating systems.

Conferences
O'Reilly brings diverse innovators together to nurture the ideas that spark revolutionary industries. We specialize in documenting the latest tools and systems, translating the innovator's knowledge into useful skills for those in the trenches. Visit *conferences.oreilly.com* for our upcoming events.

Safari Bookshelf (*safari.oreilly.com*) is the premier online reference library for programmers and IT professionals. Conduct searches across more than 1,000 books. Subscribers can zero in on answers to time-critical questions in a matter of seconds. Read the books on your Bookshelf from cover to cover or simply flip to the page you need. Try it today for free.

Visual Basic 2005 Jumpstart

Wei-Meng Lee

O'REILLY®

Beijing · Cambridge · Farnham · Köln · Paris · Sebastopol · Taipei · Tokyo

Visual Basic 2005 Jumpstart
by Wei-Meng Lee

Published by O'Reilly Media, Inc., 1005 Gravenstein Highway North, Sebastopol, CA 95472.

O'Reilly books may be purchased for educational, business, or sales promotional use. Online editions are also available for most titles (*safari.oreilly.com*). For more information, contact our corporate/institutional sales department: (800) 998-9938 or *corporate@oreilly.com*.

Editor:	John Osborn
Production Editor:	Adam Witwer
Cover Designer:	Ellie Volckhausen
Interior Designer:	David Futato

Printing History:

September 2005:   First Edition.

 This book uses RepKover™, a durable and flexible lay-flat binding.

ISBN: 0-596-10071-X
[M]

Table of Contents

Foreword vii

Preface ix

1. **Introducing Visual Basic 2005** 1
   Create the Application and Its Main Window   2
   Add a Menu and Toolbar   2
   Connect to a Database and Browse Records   6
   Create an Exit Dialog Box   13
   Handle Exit and Close Events   15
   Run and Debug the Application   18
   Inspect an Object at Runtime   20
   Add an About Box   20
   Configure the Application   24
   Summary   28

2. **Programming with Visual Basic** 29
   Data Types   29
   Variables   31
   Constants   34
   Strings   37
   Arrays   38
   Type Conversion   39
   Operators   41
   Statements   43
   Functions and Subroutines   47

Error-Handling   51
My Namespace   54
Summary   57

3. Putting Object-Oriented Programming to Work **58**
Working with Classes and Objects   59
Reusing and Customizing Classes   66
Designing Your Own Classes   81
Controlling How Classes Are Implemented   89
Summary   97

4. Developing a Windows Application **98**
Creating the Windows Application and Building the Main Window   99
Viewing Book Information Offline   121
Deploying the Application   125
Automatic Updating   130
Summary   135

5. Building Web Applications **136**
Building the Storefront   138
Creating a Shopping Cart   147
Members Area   157
Testing the Application   166
Summary   170

6. Moving from VB 6 to VB 2005 .... **171**
Migrate, Replace, Rewrite, or Reuse?   171
Using COM Objects in VB 2005   176
Upgrading VB 6 Applications   180
Summary   188

Index **189**

Foreword

Visual Basic revolutionized programming when it was first released in 1991 by making it easier than ever for developers to build Windows programs. This success continued with Visual Basic 6.0, which became one of the world's most popular programming languages. The transition from Visual Basic 6.0 to Visual Basic .NET offered developers a new range of development possibilities. Using the same set of development skills, developers could now target Windows, Web, Mobile, and Office applications better than ever before. Visual Basic 2005 is the most powerful and accessible version of Visual Basic. The addition of features like the My namespace and Edit and Continue help developers to address business problems with the productivity that is the hallmark of Visual Basic development.

This book is a great way to take your Visual Basic 6.0 development skills forward to become an expert in Visual Basic 2005 programming. I'm happy to have partnered with Wei-Meng and O'Reilly to create this book which is a part of an ongoing effort to enable Visual Basic 6.0 developers to leverage their existing skills. Experienced VB programmers will see how their existing Visual Basic skills can be applied to quickly become productive in Visual Basic 2005.

I hope that you find this book useful and look forward to hearing from you with any comments. Please feel free to contact me directly at *jroxe@microsoft.com*.

—Jay Roxe
Product Manager, Visual Basic
Microsoft Corporation

Preface

Who This Book Is For

Visual Basic 2005 Jumpstart is written for VB 6 programmers who have yet to move to Visual Basic 2005, the latest release of Microsoft Visual Basic, one of the world's most popular programming languages. With VB 2005, Microsoft has given VB 6 developers a host of reasons to upgrade now, including the return of VB 6 features omitted from earlier versions of VB.NET.

My aim is to provide you with a starting point—a jumpstart—that demonstrates how easy it is to become productive with the new language when it's paired with the Visual Studio 2005 development environment.

To get the most out of this book, you'll need a copy of Visual Studio 2005 that supports Visual Basic (see "What You Need to Use This Book"). I encourage you to work your way through the sample applications, especially those in Chapters 1, 4, and 5, as they are purposefully small and designed to show off the best of the new features in VB 2005. You'll be surprised at how easily and quickly you can build a relatively sophisticated Windows or web application. The complete source code for the book (along with any errata) is available on the O'Reilly web page for this book, *http://www.oreilly.com/catalog/vbjumpstart/*.

How This Book Is Organized

Visual Basic 2005 Jumpstart consists of six chapters, each of which focuses on a particular aspect of the VB 2005 language or a type of project that VB 6 programmers are likely to encounter in making the move to the new tool.

Chapter 1, *Introducing Visual Basic 2005*

You'll use VB 2005 and Visual Studio 2005 to build a simple Windows application that any VB 6 programmer will recognize. Though the application is simple, building it illustrates a number of powerful features present in the VB 2005 language and the Visual Studio 2005 development tool. Among these are new Windows controls with Smart Tasks, new Windows application templates, restored support for edit-and-continue, improved IntelliSense and Code Editor facilities, the Data Source Configuration Wizard, and Application Settings.

Chapter 2, *Programming with Visual Basic*

you will be taken on a whirlwind tour of the VB 2005 language and its syntax, and you'll see how it compares with that of VB 6. If you are a VB 6 programmer, you'll be happy to learn that much of what you already know is still supported (or enhanced) in VB 2005. You'll also be introduced to the My namespace, which vastly expands the trove of functions available to Visual Basic programmers and provides easier access to the rich functionality of the .NET Framework Class Library.

Chapter 3, *Putting Object-Oriented Programming to Work*

You will be introduced to the support for object-oriented programming (OOP) available in VB 2005 and will learn why it matters. A principal reason for using OOP features in VB 2005 is the support they provide for reusing, customizing, and controlling the use others make of your code, and you'll learn about a variety of techniques for accomplishing these tasks. You'll also learn about the VB 2005 Class Designer, how to extend an existing class by inheriting from it, generic classes, Partial classes, and advanced OOP concepts such as abstract classes and methods, interfaces, attributes, and access modifiers.

Chapter 4, *Developing a Windows Application*

You will build a Windows application that demonstrates the ease with which Visual Studio 2005 and VB 2005 can be used to create professional Windows applications. You will also learn how to consume web services and how data can be persisted in a SQL database, and you will see how ClickOnce makes deployment and updating of smart clients easy and effortless.

Chapter 5, *Building Web Applications*

You will build a simple e-commerce web application using new controls in ASP.NET 2.0 that let you build powerful applications without writing much VB 2005 code at all. You will see how to use a Master Page to maintain a consistent look and feel for the pages of your site. You will also see how information about users could be persisted using the new Profile service. Last but not least, you will learn how easy it is to implement security in your web applications using new ASP.NET 2.0 security controls with the Membership class that powers them.

Chapter 6, *Moving from VB 6 to VB 2005*

You will learn about the various factors that you need to consider when deciding whether to upgrade an exisitng application. Upgrading from VB 6 to VB 2005 requires careful review of the application as well as analysis of the various benefits that a migration will bring you. You will also learn how you can continue to use your legacy COM components in VB 2005 and how the new RegFree COM feature in VB 2005 shields you from the notorious DLL hell problem. Finally, the chapter ends with a demonstration of the Visual Basic 6.0 Code Advisor and the Upgrade Wizard, which aim to ease the upgrade of your existing VB 6 applications to VB 2005, should you decide to go that route.

What You Need to Use This Book

To try out the many hands-on projects and code samples in this book, you'll need to install any edition of Visual Studio 2005 on a computer running Windows. You can also use a combination of the new Visual Studio Express Editions. To work your way through all of the examples, you'll need to install Visual Basic 2005 Express Edition, Visual Web Developer 2005 Express Edition, and SQL Server 2005 Express Edition, all of which are available on the MSDN web site.

Conventions Used in This Book

The following typographical conventions are used in this book:

Plain text

Indicates menu titles, menu options, menu buttons, and keyboard accelerators (such as Alt and Ctrl).

Italic

Indicates new terms, URLs, email addresses, filenames, file extensions, pathnames, directories, and Unix utilities.

Constant width

Indicates commands, options, switches, variables, attributes, keys, functions, types, controls, classes, namespaces, methods, modules, properties, parameters, values, objects, events, event handlers, XML tags, HTML tags, macros, the contents of files, or the output from commands.

Constant width bold

> Shows commands or other text that should be typed literally by the user. Bold is also used in code samples to highlight lines of code that are discussed in the text.

Constant width italic

> Shows text that should be replaced with user-supplied values.

> This icon signifies a tip, suggestion, or general note.

> This icon indicates a warning or caution.

Using Code Examples

This book is here to help you get your job done. In general, you may use the code in this book in your programs and documentation. You do not need to contact us for permission unless you're reproducing a significant portion of the code. For example, writing a program that uses several chunks of code from this book does not require permission. Selling or distributing a CD-ROM of examples from O'Reilly books *does* require permission. Answering a question by citing this book and quoting example code does not require permission. Incorporating a significant amount of example code from this book into your product's documentation *does* require permission.

We appreciate, but do not require, attribution. An attribution usually includes the title, author, publisher, and ISBN. For example: "*Visual Basic 2005 Jumpstart*, by Wei-Meng Lee. Copyright 2005 O'Reilly Media, Inc., 0-596-10071-X."

If you feel your use of code examples falls outside fair use or the permission given above, feel free to contact us at *permissions@oreilly.com*.

Safari Enabled

Safari When you see a Safari® Enabled icon on the cover of your **BOOKS ONLINE** favorite technology book, that means the book is available **ENABLED** online through the O'Reilly Network Safari Bookshelf.

Safari offers a solution that's better than e-books. It's a virtual library that lets you easily search thousands of top tech books, cut and paste code samples, download chapters, and find quick answers when you need the most accurate, current information. Try it for free at *http://safari.oreilly.com*.

I'd Like to Hear from You

Please send comments, suggestions, and errata to *wei_meng_lee@hotmail.com*. You can also visit my web site at: *http://www.developerlearningsolutions.com* for a list of articles that I have written on .NET. Check out the Code Library section to download sample code for topics on .NET, VB 2005, ASP.NET 2.0, and the .NET Compact Framework.

Comments and Questions

Please address comments and questions concerning this book to the publisher:

O'Reilly Media, Inc.
1005 Gravenstein Highway North
Sebastopol, CA 95472
(800) 998-9938 (in the United States or Canada)
(707) 829-0515 (international or local)
(707) 829-0104 (fax)

We have a web page for this book, where we list errata, examples, and any additional information. You can access this page at:

http://www.oreilly.com/catalog/vbjumpstart/

To comment or ask technical questions about this book, send email to:

bookquestions@oreilly.com

For more information about our books, conferences, Resource Centers, and the O'Reilly Network, see our web site at:

http://www.oreilly.com

Acknowledgments

I am very grateful to my editor, John Osborn, for giving me this opportunity to write a book on VB 2005. His patience and attention to detail have definitely made this book a better read. John has painstakingly read and reread every single word I have written and has always challenged me to rethink what I have written, and for this I am much honored to work with John. A big thank you, John!

Special thanks are also due to Jay Roxe, Product Manager of Visual Basic at Microsoft, for his support and review of this book. Jay has played an instrumental role in shaping the outline of this book and provided many useful suggestions for improving its content. Thanks for the hard work, Jay!

I also wish to express my gratitude to the reviewers for their comments and numerous suggestions. They include Robert Green, Jeff Barr, Paul Yuknewicz, and Joseph Binder.

As always, it has been a pleasure working with the O'Reilly team. A big thank you to the unsung heroes behind the scenes that made this book possible. Thanks!

CHAPTER 1

Introducing Visual Basic 2005

When Microsoft released its new version of Visual Basic in 2002, many developers willingly upgraded to take advantage of the new web functionality, security, and performance provided by the .NET platform on which it was built. But in doing so, many also felt they were leaving behind the features that had made Visual Basic 6.0 such a popular tool for the rapid development of Windows applications in the first place.

The release of Visual Basic 2005 (VB 2005) is in many ways a return to Visual Basic's roots as the Rapid Application Development (RAD) tool of choice. Many of the most popular features of earlier versions are back, such as Edit and Continue, along with dozens of new controls, better IntelliSense, an improved debugger, and a host of other tools that speed up programming, debugging, testing, and deployment.

Besides the many tools added to its interactive development environment (IDE), Visual Basic 2005 provides more support than ever for developing the next generation of network-enabled Windows clients and web applications, while a new set of functionality unique to VB 2005—the My namespace— gives you the means by which to perform many common tasks without having to work your way through the complex types of the .NET class libraries.

The best way to learn about Visual Studio 2005 is by using the tool to build an application. In the following sections, you'll assemble a straightforward Windows client that enables users to connect to a database and browse or update the information they find there. You'll work with the *authors* table of the *pub's* database that ships with SQL Server 2005. You'll also see how you can extend the application using some of the features new to VB 2005, such as project templates and application configuration tools. Figure 1-1 shows how the main window of the the completed application will look when you've finished your work.

Although this book uses Microsoft Visual Studio 2005 as the tool to build the sample applications, you can also use Microsoft Visual Basic 2005 Express Edition.

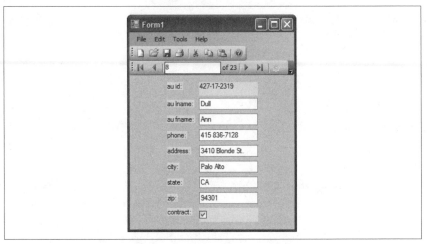

Figure 1-1. The completed pubs database Windows client

Create the Application and Its Main Window

Let's start by using Visual Studio 2005 to create a Windows application, one that you can program with VB 2005.

1. First, you need to fire up Visual Studio 2005 and open a new project by selecting File → New Project... on the Visual Studio 2005 menu. Visual Studio displays the New Project dialog shown in Figure 1-2.

2. In the Project types window of the New Project dialog, select Visual Basic and then select the Windows Application template in the Visual Studio installed templates dialog window. Keep the default project Name, WindowsApplication1, provided by Visual Studio. Click OK.

   Visual Studio 2005 will present you with its familiar Windows development environment, shown in Figure 1-3, including a designer surface for Form1, which will become the startup window of your application.

Add a Menu and Toolbar

Let's now add a menu and toolbar to the form. In VB 2005, you can create professional looking Windows applications, complete with menus and toolbars that look like those used with Microsoft Office applications.

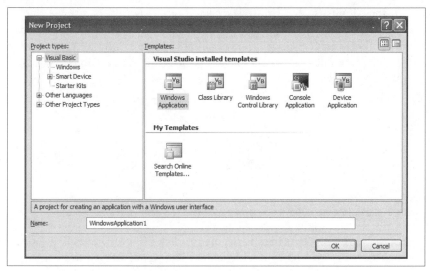

Figure 1-2. Creating a new Windows application

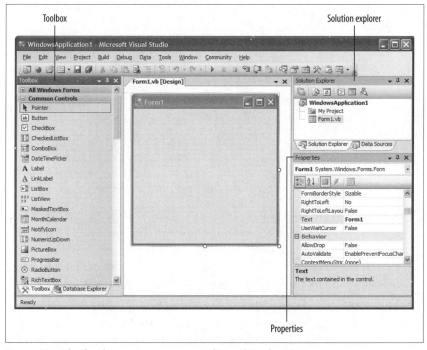

Figure 1-3. The development environment of Visual Studio 2005

1. In the Menus & Toolbars tab in Toolbox, shown in Figure 1-4, locate and then drag and drop the ToolStripContainer control onto the form. The ToolStripContainer control allows other controls (such as the ToolStrip control) to anchor in the four positions available (left, right, top, and bottom).

Figure 1-4. The various controls under the Menus & Toolbars tab in Toolbox

In the ToolStripContainer Tasks menu, click on the "Dock Fill in Form" link (see Figure 1-5) to dock the ToolStripContainer control onto the form. This will cause the ToolStripContainer control to fill up the entire form and automatically resize itself when the form is resized.

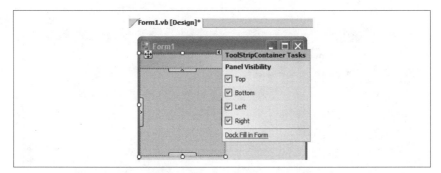

Figure 1-5. Filling the entire form with the ToolStripContainer control

2. Now you'll add the application menu. Double-click on the MenuStrip control in the Toolbox to add it to the form. The MenuStrip control displays a standard list of drop-down menus at the top of a window. In the MenuStrip Tasks menu, click on the Insert Standard Items link to add a list of commonly used menu items to the control (see Figure 1-6).

Your form should now look like the one shown in Figure 1-7.

Now you'll add a toolbar to Form1. Select the MenuStrip control that you have just added by single-clicking on it. In the Toolbox, double click on the ToolStrip control (or drag and drop it) to add it to the form. This will add the ToolStrip control to the top of the ToolStripContainer control, thereby making it moveable. You use the ToolStrip control to display buttons for tasks users will commonly want

Figure 1-6. Inserting standard menu items into the MenuStrip control

Figure 1-7. The MenuStrip control

to perform. Initially, the toolbar is blank. To add common toolbar items, click on the Insert Standard Items link in the ToolStrip Tasks menus. Your form should now look like Figure 1-8.

Figure 1-8. The MenuStrip and ToolStrip controls

3. To test the application, press F5. You will now be able to drag the ToolStrip control and anchor it in one of the four positions (see Figure 1-9).

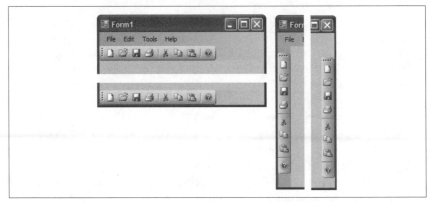

Figure 1-9. Anchoring the ToolStrip control in various positions

Connect to a Database and Browse Records

One great time-saving feature in VB 2005 is its new support for automatic data binding. The automatic–data binding feature allows you to connect to a data source and then drag and drop the connection onto a Windows Forms application. A set of controls bound to the data source will then be automatically added to the form, and you can perform a variety of operations on the data source, such as navigating through records, searching for a specific record, and more, without having to write any code.

To see how automatic data binding works, you will now connect to a database and then drag and drop one of its tables onto your form so that you can view and work with its records. You will use SQL Server 2005 Express and the *pubs* database and then view and edit the records in the *authors* table.

1. Select Data → Show Data Sources to display the Data Sources window, as shown in Figure 1-10. The Data Sources window allows you to connect to your data sources (such as databases, web services, and business objects) and view their content. Click on the Add New Data Source... link to add a new data source to your project (see Figure 1-10).

    When the Data Source Configuration Wizard appears, click Next.

2. The Choose a Data Source dialog, which appears next, lets you choose between a database, a web service, or some other object as the source of your data. You'll be using a database, so click the Database icon and then click Next.

3. Now you need to select a data connection to use to connect to your database. In the "Choose your data connection" dialog, click New Connection....

Figure 1-10. The Data Sources window

4. The Add Connection dialog will be shown (see Figure 1-11).

> For this step, I am assuming you have SQL Server 2005 Express installed on your computer. You can download SQL Server 2005 Express from: *http://www.microsoft.com/sql/ express/default.mspx.*
>
> As SQL Server 2005 Express does not come with any sample databases, you need to install the sample database yourself. See the sidebar "SQL Server 2005 Express and the pubs and Northwind Databases" for more information.

Enter the details of your database (see Figure 1-11). Type `.\SQLEXPRESS` for Server name if your database is installed locally on your machine. Select the database to use (in this example, select the sample *pubs* database in SQL Server 2005 Express). Click OK and Next in the next window.

5. Visual Studio 2005 now has the information it needs to create the connection string that will let your application access the *pubs* database. The "Save the connection string to the application configuration file" step gives you the useful option of naming and saving the connection string in the application configuration file, as shown in Figure 1-12. Having the information in a configuration file lets you change database details without recompiling the application, even after it has been deployed. Leave the checkbox checked, give the connection string the name `pubsConnectionString`, and click Next to display the next part of the Data Source Configuration Wizard dialog.

6. With a connection string in place, you're now in a position to select the table(s) you want to work with. The "Choose your database objects" step shown in Figure 1-13 displays the tables (and fields) of the *pubs*

Figure 1-11. Adding a new database connection

SQL Server 2005 Express and the pubs and Northwind Databases

SQL Server 2005 Express does not ship with the *pubs* and *Northwind* sample databases. But you can install them by downloading the *pubs* and *Northwind* database installation scripts at *http://www.microsoft.com/downloads/details. aspx?familyid=06616212-0356-46a0-8da2-eebc53a68034&displaylang=en.*

Once the scripts are installed on your system, go to the Visual Studio 2005 command prompt (Start → Programs → Microsoft Visual Studio 2005 → Visual Studio Tools → Visual Studio 2005 Command Prompt) and change to the directory containing your installation scripts (assuming your installation scripts are stored in *C:*). Type in the following to install the *pubs* and *Northwind* databases:

```
C:\>sqlcmd -S .\SQLEXPRESS -i instpubs.sql
C:\>sqlcmd -S .\SQLEXPRESS -i instnwnd.sql
```

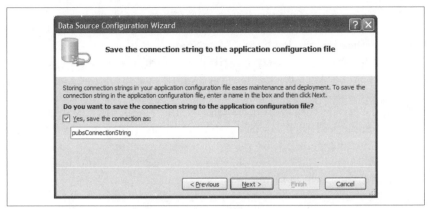

Figure 1-12. Saving the connection string in the application configuration file

database. Your application will give users access to author information stored in the *pubs* database, so check the *authors* table to select all fields and then click Finish to move to the next step, which displays a completed Data Sources window for your application. You can return to the Data Sources window whenever you need to make changes by clicking on the Data Sources tab next to the Solution Explorer or by going to the Visual Studio menu and selecting Data → Show Data Sources.

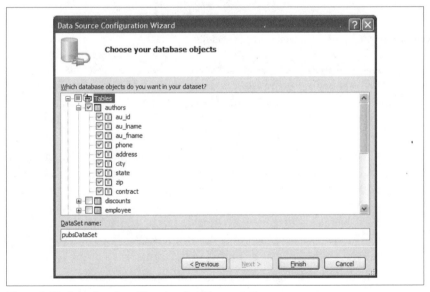

Figure 1-13. Selecting the table to work with

7. One last step is required to make the *authors* table accessible to your users: you need to bind each field to a control that can be displayed in the application window. In the Data Sources window, you'll see that the *authors* table is displayed as a tree, as shown in Figure 1-14, and that each field has been bound to a specific type of control. For example, the *au_lname* field is bound to a text box (represented by the icon containing the letters "abl"). You can change the binding by clicking on the field name and then choosing another binding. For now, we'll make only one change. Click on the drop-down menu for the *au_id* field and then choose the Label control (as represented by the icon containing the letter A, as shown in Figure 1-14).

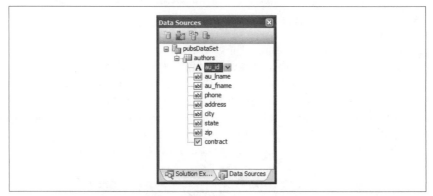

Figure 1-14. Changing the bindings of the fields

Also, you should change the *authors* table binding to *Details* (using the drop-down menu for the *authors* field shown in Figure 1-15) so that you can view the *authors* table one record at a time. The reason for doing this will become evident to you in the next step when we add the ability for users to navigate through the table.

Now you're ready the drag and drop the *authors* item in the Data Sources window onto the default Windows Form and watch Visual Studio 2005 perform some real magic. For starters, Visual Studio automatically populates Form1 with the controls shown in Figure 1-16. Visual Studio 2005 also adds a new BindingNavigator control to the top of the form. The new BindingNavigator control lets users navigate through all the records in the table as displayed in the form.

8. By default, the BindingNavigator control is docked (fixed) to the top of the form and is not moveable. Set the Dock property to None and rearrange the controls as shown in Figure 1-17.

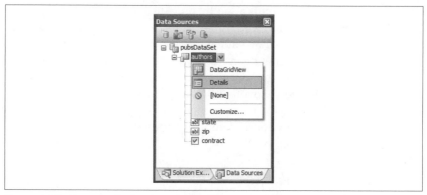

Figure 1-15. Changing the binding of the table

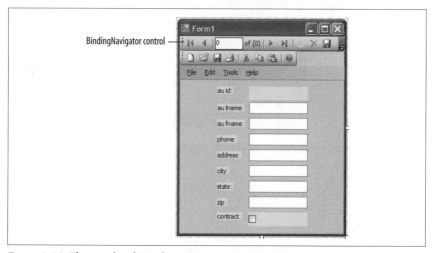

Figure 1-16. The populated Windows Form

 You can rearrange the BindingNavigator control by increasing the size of the ToolStripContainer control. Simply click the arrow shown at the top of the ToolStripContainer control.

Figure 1-17. Arranging the controls at the top of the Form

9. You can now test the application by pressing F5. Form1, the main window of your application, will display, complete with menu, toolbar, and navigation control, as shown in Figure 1-18. You should be able to navigate the records in the *authors* table as well as move the various toolbars around. Try scrolling through the table by clicking the arrows on the BindingNavigator control.

Figure 1-18. Navigating the records in the table

You should also be able to edit individual records by modifying the values in the text box bound to each field. Try it. To save a modified record to the database, you need to click on the Save icon, which is represented by the diskette icon in the BindingNavigator control.

Visual Studio 2005 automatically adds the relevant code to the code behind of the form to handle the retrieving and saving of data. To see the code added by Visual Studio 2005, double-click on the diskette icon to reveal the code behind. You will see the code shown in Example 1-1.

Example 1-1. Save menu item code behind added by Visual Studio 2005

```
Private Sub bindingNavigatorSaveItem_Click( _
    ByVal sender As System.Object, _
    ByVal e As System.EventArgs) _
    Handles bindingNavigatorSaveItem.Click
    If Me.Validate Then
        Me.AuthorsBindingSource.EndEdit( )
        Me.AuthorsTableAdapter.Update(Me.PubsDataSet.authors)
    Else
        System.Windows.Forms.MessageBox.Show( _
            Me, "Validation errors occurred.", "Save", _
            System.Windows.Forms.MessageBoxButtons.OK, _
```

```
            System.Windows.Forms.MessageBoxIcon.Warning)
      End If

End Sub
```

Create an Exit Dialog Box

For most Windows applications, it is customary to ask users if they really want to quit an application when they either click the Close window button or select Exit on the File menu. In this section, you'll use Visual Studio 2005 and VB 2005 to add a dialog box that asks users to confirm that they really want to quit the application when they select either action.

1. First, let's create the dialog box by adding a new Dialog to the project. You add a new Dialog to your project by right-clicking on the project name in Solution Explorer, which is `WindowsApplication1`, and then selecting Add → New Item.... In the Add New Item dialog, select Dialog and use the default name of *Dialog1.vb* as shown in Figure 1-19.

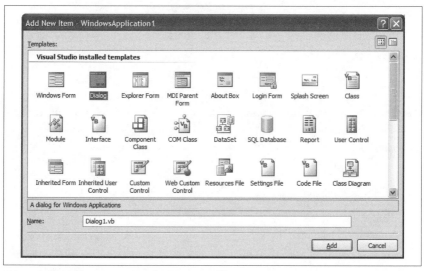

Figure 1-19. Adding a new Windows Form to the project

2. Notice that the Dialog window already comes with two buttons: OK (`OK_Button`) and Cancel (`Cancel_Button`).

3. Populate the dialog with the `Label` control shown in Figure 1-20 by dragging and dropping it from the Toolbox. Also, resize the dialog window.

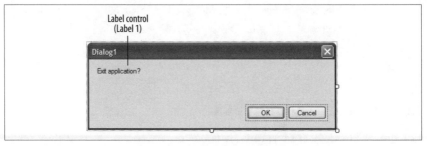

Label control
(Label 1)

Dialog1   ☒

Exit application?

                                    OK   Cancel

Figure 1-20. Populating the dialog window with the Label control

Snaplines

One of the most visible enhancements in Windows Forms 2.0 is the snaplines that are automatically shown when you drag and drop a control onto a form. Using snaplines, you can position controls on your form so that they are evenly spaced out. The figure shows snaplines in action when you try to position the Label control.

4. Set the properties of the various controls to the values shown in Table 1-1. To set the properties of a control, right-click the control and select Properties to display its Property window. Look for each Property you wish to set by scrolling through the Properties window and entering the appropriate value.

Table 1-1. Properties of the various controls

Control	Property	Value	Comments
Dialog1	Text	Exit	Changes the title of the Windows Form
Dialog1	AcceptButton	OK_Button	Sets the OK button to the default button of the form so that it is clicked when the user presses the Enter key.
			Note that this has already been set for you by Visual Studio 2005.
Dialog1	CancelButton	Cancel_ Button	Sets the Cancel button to be activated when the user presses the Esc key.
			Note that this has already been set for you by Visual Studio 2005.

Table 1-1. Properties of the various controls (continued)

Control	Property	Value	Comments
OK_Button	DialogResult	OK	Sets the OK button to the value of OK for the dialog result.
Cancel_Button	DialogResult	Cancel	Sets the Cancel button to the value of Cancel for thedialog result.

Handle Exit and Close Events

Now it's time to write some code to link the Exit dialog with the events triggered by users when they attempt to exit or close the application.

1. First, you'll add code to deal with the Exit menu item when a user selects it. To get started, expand the File menu in Form1 and double-click on the Exit menu item (see Figure 1-21) to open the code-behind page shown in Figure 1-22.

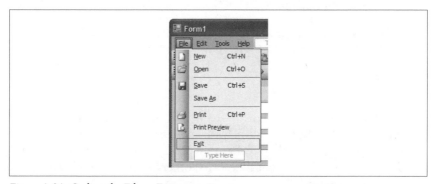

Figure 1-21. Coding the File → Exit menu item

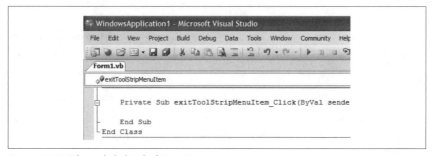

Figure 1-22. The code behind of Form1

The code-behind page contains all of the code that you write for the application. So far in this chapter, all of the work has been done by Visual Studio, but the code it has generated to support your work with the designer and wizards is hidden and out of sight for now. You'll see how to view this code in Chapter 2.

When you double-click on the Exit item of the application menu on Form1, Visual Studio deduces that you wish to write code to specify how the exit event will be handled, just as it does in VB 6. Note that the code behind page in this example is named *Form1.vb*. As you can see in Figure 1-22, Visual Studio has already generated the code to create the event handler. All you need to do is specify what specific actions are to be taken when the event handler is called by placing your cursor on the line below the handler declaration and entering your own code.

2. Now, code the exit event of the ToolStrip control by entering the code shown in bold in Example 1-2 on the code-behind page.

Example 1-2. Exit menu item event handler

```
Private Sub exitToolStripMenuItem_Click( _
    ByVal sender As System.Object, _
    ByVal e As System.EventArgs) _
    Handles exitToolStripMenuItem.Click
    Dim result As DialogResult = Dialog1.ShowDialog()
    If result = Windows.Forms.DialogResult.OK Then
        End
    End If
End Sub
```

When users select the Exit item on the File menu, an exit event fires and the code in Example 1-2 displays Dialog1, which forces users to confirm whether or not they really want to exit the application. If a user selects OK, then the application exits; otherwise, no action is taken and the dialog window closes.

Much of the code in Example 1-2 will seem familiar to VB 6 users. Dim statements are still used to declare variables, the If...Then statement is unchanged, and the Sub...End Sub block is still used to define subroutines. What's new is the way in which the code makes use of classes, methods, and properties found in the .NET Framework, most visibly in the use of dot (.) syntax to reference them. You'll learn more about VB 2005 data types and language syntax in Chapter 2. Later in Chapter 3, you'll see how to use the new support for object-oriented programming and the .NET Framework in VB 2005 to greatly increase your productivity.

3. Now you need to add code to handle the case when the user closes the application window (Form1) by clicking on the Close button at top the right of the application windowt. This is handled by coding the FormClosing event of Form1, as shown in Example 1-3. Again, when the

Sideline Coloring

The IDE in Visual Studio 2005 uses sideline coloring to highlight the lines that you have changed. The figure below shows the different colors that are displayed to the left of the code edit window after you enter the bold code in Example 1-2.

The green color means that the lines have been modified and saved in the current edit session.

The yellow color signifies that the lines have been changed but have not yet been saved. When you save the project or run the application, the yellow coding will turn green. When the project is closed and opened again in Visual Studio 2005, the green coding will disappear.

Note that sideline coloring is activated only if the Track Changes option is set. By default, it is set on in the Visual Studio 2005/Team System Beta, but it is not set by default in VB Express.

```
              Private Sub exitToolStripMenuItem_Click(ByVal sender As System.Object,
Green ────        Dim result As DialogResult = Dialog1.ShowDialog()
                  If result = Windows.Forms.DialogResult.OK Then
Yellow ───            End
                  End If
Green ────    End Sub
            End Class
```

user clicks the Close button, you'll display Dialog1. If the user selects the OK button, end the application. If the user selects the Cancel button, cancel the close operation by setting the `Cancel` property of the `System.Windows.Forms.FormClosingEventArgs` argument to `True`. You can get Visual Studio 2005 to generate the code stub for the `FormClosing` event by selecting the Form1 Events item in the left drop-down list (see Figure 1-23) and then selecting `FormClosing` in the second drop-down list. Enter the code shown in bold in Example 1-3.

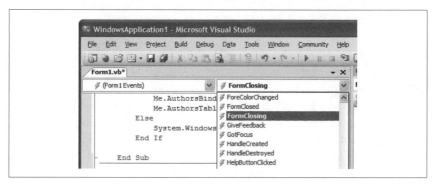

Figure 1-23. Generating the code stub for the FormClosing event

Example 1-3. FormClosing event handler

```
Private Sub Form1_FormClosing( _
    ByVal sender As Object, _
    ByVal e As System.Windows.Forms.FormClosingEventArgs) _
    Handles Me.FormClosing
        Dim result As DialogResult = Dialog1.ShowDialog( )
        If result = Windows.Forms.DialogResult.OK Then
            End
        Else
            e.Cancel = True
        End If
End Sub
```

Improved IntelliSense

One of the most useful features of VB 2005 is the IntelliSense feature in Visual Studio. IntelliSense greatly reduces the amount of memorizing you need to do and automatically completes statements as you type.

IntelliSense now performs smart filtering to list only the relevant methods, properties, and events of objects into two tabs—Common and All—so that you can quickly access the commonly used properties, methods, and events of an object without having to wade through the entire list (see figure).

This improvement reduces the number of items showing up in an IntelliSense list, thereby making it easier for developers to search for what they want. If what you need cannot be found on the Common tab, you can always click on the All tab to see the complete list.

```
Private Sub Form1_FormClosing(ByVal sender As Object, ByVal e As Syst
    Dim result As DialogResult = Dialog1.ShowDialog()
    If result = Windows.Forms.DialogResult.OK Then
        End
    Else
        e.
    End
End Sub
```

| Cancel | Public Property Cancel() As Boolean |
| CloseReason | Gets or sets a value indicating whether the event should be canceled. |

| Common | All |

Run and Debug the Application

With the code you have added in the last section, it is now time to test the application. This is a good chance for you to see some of the new enhancements in the new Visual Studio 2005 debugger. For this example, you will set a breakpoint so that you can examine the values of variables at a particular point in the code.

1. Now set a breakpoint in the application by clicking on the gray bar on the left of the code edit window (see Figure 1-24) and then running the application by pressing F5. You will set the breakpoint so that the program halts when you click on the Close box, allowing you to examine the value of DialogResult returned by the Exit dialog box (Dialog1).

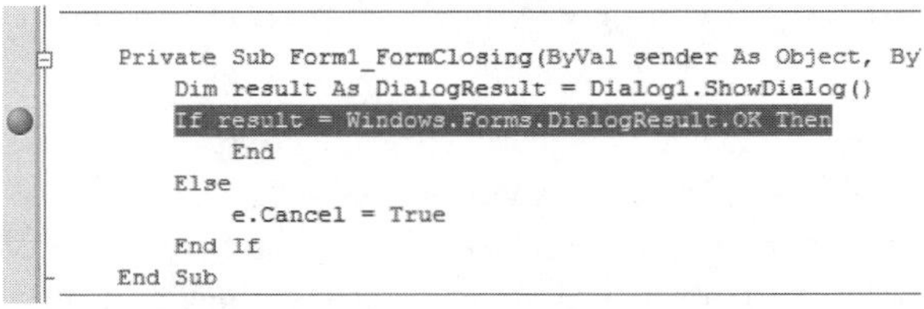

```
Private Sub Form1_FormClosing(ByVal sender As Object, By
    Dim result As DialogResult = Dialog1.ShowDialog()
    If result = Windows.Forms.DialogResult.OK Then
        End
    Else
        e.Cancel = True
    End If
End Sub
```

Figure 1-24. Setting a breakpoint

2. When the form is loaded, close the form to display the dialog box. Click OK, and the application will stop at the breakpoint you have set. To step through the code one line at a time, press F11 (see Figure 1-25).

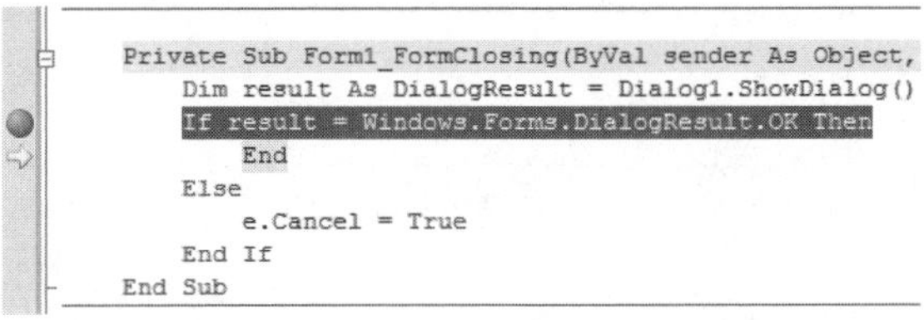

```
Private Sub Form1_FormClosing(ByVal sender As Object,
    Dim result As DialogResult = Dialog1.ShowDialog()
    If result = Windows.Forms.DialogResult.OK Then
        End
    Else
        e.Cancel = True
    End If
End Sub
```

Figure 1-25. Stepping through the code

Edit and Continue

Yes! The edit-and-continue feature that VB 6 programmers have always taken for granted is supported in VB 2005. Using the edit-and-continue feature, programmers can set breakpoints using the debugger in Visual Studio and then make changes on the fly (you can even roll back execution steps). After the changes are made, the application can continue executing without the need to stop entirely and recompile.

Inspect an Object at Runtime

The debugger in Visual Studio 2005 now supports a new feature known as DataTips. Using DataTips, you can examine the values in a complex data type while you are debugging the application, otherwise known as *debug time*. This is a marked improvement over Visual Studio .NET 2003, where only simple data types can be examined by placing the cursor over a variable name.

Figure 1-26 shows the DataTips display for the FormClosingEventArgs object. To see this result, simply position your cursor over the name of the variable or object that you are interested in while the program is stopped at a breakpoint. Not only can you view the values of variables and objects, you can also edit and change their values during debug time.

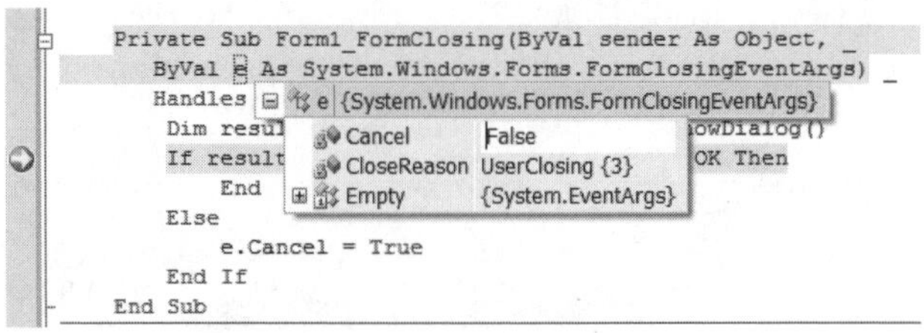

```
Private Sub Form1_FormClosing(ByVal sender As Object, _
    ByVal e As System.Windows.Forms.FormClosingEventArgs) _
    Handles  e {System.Windows.Forms.FormClosingEventArgs}
    Dim resul        owDialog()
    If result   Cancel        False              OK Then
        End     CloseReason   UserClosing {3}
    Else        Empty         {System.EventArgs}
            e.Cancel = True
    End If
End Sub
```

Figure 1-26. Using the DataTips in Visual Studio 2005

Add an About Box

VB 2005 now comes with several new templates that make developing a Windows application easy. Among the new templates are:

Explorer Form
   Allows you to build applications similar to Windows Explorer, with a tree-like display on the left pane and a detailed view on the right pane.

About Box
   Displays an About window listing detailed information (such as version number, copyright, credits, etc.) about the current application.

Login Form
   Creates a standard login window to simplify the task of user authentication.

Splash Screen
   Displays a welcome screen when your application is launched.

In this section, you will add an About box to your application using the About Box template. The About box for an application is displayed when a user selects Help → About... and contains useful information about the application, including its manufacturer and version number. Much of the information in the About box is available from the application and its configuration files.

1. First, you need to create an About box form. Right-click on the project name (WindowsApplication1) in Solution Explorer and select Add New Item.... Select the About Box template and accept the default name of *AboutBox1.vb* provided by Visual Studio 2005. Click Add (see Figure 1-27).

Figure 1-27. Adding an About box to the project

The *AboutBox1.vb* form will be added to your project, and Visual Studio 2005 will display a designer for the feature as shown in Figure 1-28.

2. Let's personalize the form by adding an image of the cover for this book to replace the default pretzel-like image. Click the LogoPictureBox control and then, in the Property window for the control, click the "..." button of its Image property. This will display the Select Resource dialog window. Click the Import... button of the dialog to select your own image for the About box (*C:\vbjumpstartpg.gif*). Click OK (see Figure 1-29).

Figure 1-28. The controls on the AboutBox1 window

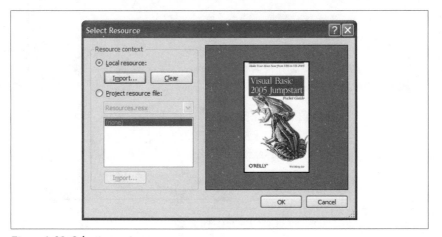

Figure 1-29. Selecting an image resource

 You can download the *vbjumpstartpg.gif* image from: *http://www.oreilly.com/catalog/vbjumpstart/*.

3. Set the SizeMode property of the LogoPictureBox control to CenterImage.

4. To configure the information about your application so that it can be displayed by the About box, right-click on the project name in Solution Explorer and then select Properties. In the Application tab, click on the Assembly Information... button (see Figure 1-30).

5. Set the information as shown in Figure 1-31.

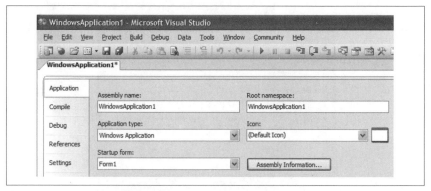

Figure 1-30. Configuring project information

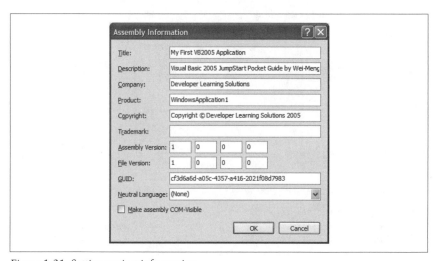

Figure 1-31. Setting project information

6. The AboutBox1 window should now look like the one shown in Figure 1-32.

7. To link Form1 with the AboutBox1 window, expand the Help menu and double-click on the About... menu item (see Figure 1-33) to open the code-behind page for Form1 and generate a code stub for the About box selection event handler.

8. Now add the line of code shown in bold to the code stub generated by Visual Studio, as shown in Example 1-4). You use the ShowDialog method of the dialog window to get the object display itself.

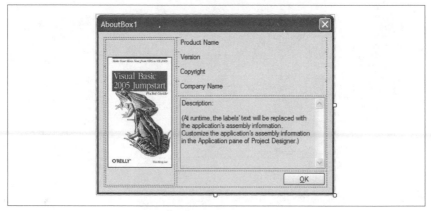

Figure 1-32. The AboutBox1 window

Figure 1-33. Coding the Help → About... menu item

Example 1-4. Help About... menu selection event handler

```
Private Sub aboutToolStripMenuItem_Click( _
    ByVal sender As System.Object, _
    ByVal e As System.EventArgs) _
    Handles aboutToolStripMenuItem.Click
    AboutBox1.ShowDialog( )
End Sub
```

9. Finally, it's time to take your work for a trial run. Press F5 to run the application. Click Help → About... and you will see the About box shown in Figure 1-34.

Configure the Application

In the application that you have built, you can move and anchor the ToolStrip control as you wish while you are using the application. However, you may have noticed that its position is lost each time you exit the application. This is because you need to manually save its positions each

BUSINESS REPLY MAIL

FIRST-CLASS MAIL   PERMIT NO. 80   SEBASTOPOL CA

Postage will be paid by addressee

O'REILLY MEDIA INC.
BOOK REGISTRATION
1005 GRAVENSTEIN HIGHWAY NORTH
SEBASTOPOL CA 95472-9910

Register Your O'Reilly Book!
oreilly.com/go/register

Register your books to receive important updates, upgrade offers and our catalog. Go to *oreilly.com/go/register*, or complete and return this postage paid card.

Name

Company/Organization

Address

City   State   Zip/Postal Code   Country

Email address   Telephone

Book Title   ISBN #

Book Title   ISBN #

Book Title   ISBN #

oreilly.com/go/register

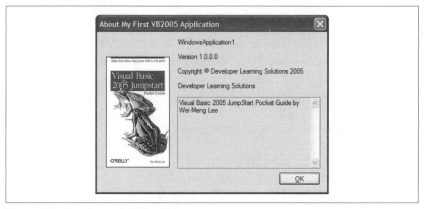

Figure 1-34. Displaying the About box

time you exit the application, or else the information will be lost. Fortunately, this can be done easily with the new Application Settings feature in VB 2005. In this section, you'll see how.

Application Settings

In VB 2005, you can now save the state of your application. For example, if a user resizes your application window, then your application can "remember" the last displayed size, if you take the appropriate steps. Using the new Application Settings feature in Windows Forms 2.0, you can create application settings for your application and then bind your controls (including Windows Forms) to these application settings via the Properties window.

---

1. You'll begin by adding code to save the location of the ToolStrip control. Select the ToolStrip control and, in its Properties window, select the PropertyBinding property (under the "(ApplicationSettings)" property; see Figure 1-35). Click the "..." button.

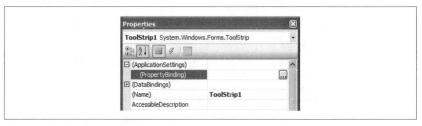

Figure 1-35. Binding application settings

2. Locate the Location property (this property determines where the control should be placed) and click the drop-down listbox. Click on the New... link at the bottom and create a new application setting called ToolStripLocation (see Figure 1-36). Be sure to set the scope to User. Click OK. Be sure to set the Location property to the newly created application setting.

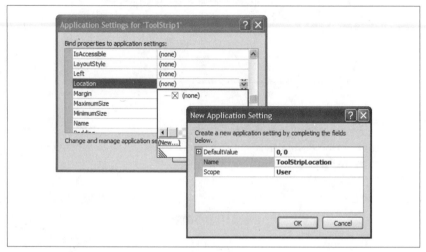

Figure 1-36. Creating the new application setting

You have now created an application setting that binds the position of the ToolStrip control to the ToolStripLocation application setting. When the form is loaded, the ToolStrip control will get its Location property from the application settings, which is saved in the *app.config* file.

 The *app.config* file contains configuration settings pertaining to your project, such as database connection strings, application logfiles, etc. It is beyond the scope of this book to discuss the *app.config* file in detail.

3. Now, perform the same steps 1 and 2 for the MenuStrip control, MenuStrip1. Name its application setting MenuLocation.

4. You will want to save the current locations of all two controls whenever Form1 is closed, so add the bold code to the FormClosing event and Exit menu item event as shown in Example 1-5.

Example 1-5. Saving control location data when a user exits or closes Form1

```
Private Sub Form1_FormClosing(ByVal sender As Object, _
    ByVal e As System.Windows.Forms.FormClosingEventArgs) _
    Handles Me.FormClosing
    Dim result As DialogResult = Dialog1.ShowDialog( )
    If result = Windows.Forms.DialogResult.OK Then
        My.Settings.MenuLocation = MenuStrip1.Location
        My.Settings.ToolStripLocation = ToolStrip1.Location
        My.Settings.Save( )
        End
    Else
        e.Cancel = True
    End If
End Sub

Private Sub exitToolStripMenuItem_Click( _
    ByVal sender As System.Object, _
    ByVal e As System.EventArgs) _
    Handles exitToolStripMenuItem.Click
    Dim result As DialogResult = Dialog1.ShowDialog( )
    If result = Windows.Forms.DialogResult.OK Then
        My.Settings.MenuLocation = MenuStrip1.Location
        My.Settings.ToolStripLocation = ToolStrip1.Location
        My.Settings.Save( )
        End
    End If
End Sub
```

 Note that in this example, only the ToolStrip control is moveable. You can make the MenuStrip control moveable by changing its GripStyle property from Hidden to Visible.

In Example 1-5, when a user closes the application either by closing the window or clicking on the Exit menu item, the application saves the position of the MenuStrip and ToolStrip controls using the application settings that you have created. You can access the application settings programmatically by using the My.Settings object (they automatically appear under the My. Settings object after you have created them). Once the locations of these two controls are assigned to the application settings, you use the Save method of the My.Setting object to persist this information to the *app.config* file.

The My Namespace

The use of My.Settings in Example 1-5 demonstrates one of the most useful and unique additions to VB 2005, the new My namespace, which encapsulates some of the most common functionalities that developers need for their daily work. The My namespace exposes several different objects, which you can observe by going to the code-behind page (*Form1.vb*) and typing **My.**. IntelliSense shows the objects of the My namespace as shown in the figure.

The aim of the My namespace is to provide direct access to commonly used libraries in the .NET Framework that were previously difficult to access. The intuitive hierarchy of the My namespace provides a mechanism that VB 2005 developers can use to easily navigate the .NET Framework class libraries and locate the classes required to perform a particular task. For example, suppose you want to play an audio file in your application. But which class should you use? Using the My namespace, it is easy to locate the right class to use. As it turns out, the class to use can be found in My.Computer.Audio.Play!

You will learn more about the My namespace in Chapter 2.

Summary

In this chapter, you built a Windows application using VB 2005 and Visual Studio 2005. Though the application is simple, its assembly illustrates several key enhancements to the VB 2005 language and the Visual Studio 2005 development tool. To recap, here are the major features you explored:

- New controls with Smart Tasks menus
- New Windows application templates
- Debugging and restored support for edit-and-continue
- Improved IntelliSense and improved Code Editor
- Data Source Configuration Wizard
- Application Settings

In next chapter, you will learn more about the language syntax of the new VB 2005.

CHAPTER 2

Programming with Visual Basic

The Visual Basic 2005 IDE is a powerful RAD tool, but as you saw in Chapter 1, sooner or later you have to roll up your sleeves and write some code, whether it's to handle a simple button event or perform a complex series of calculations on stored data. In this chapter, you'll take a look at the syntax of the VB 2005 language itself. While VB 2005 is a member in good standing of the .NET family of languages, it retains much of the flavor of its VB 6 lineage. This chapter will get you quickly up to speed with VB 2005 language and along the way will show you how some of its features have changed from those of VB 6.

Data Types

Table 2-1 lists the data types supported by VB 2005 and their counterparts in VB 6. If the size of a VB 6 type differs from that of its corresponding VB 2005 type, its size in bytes is shown in parentheses. For example, the Currency type (which takes up 8 bytes) in VB 6 is replaced in VB 2005 by the Decimal type. The old Decimal type (which takes up 12 bytes in VB 6), is now 16 bytes. Integer is now 4 bytes, instead of its 2 bytes in VB 6. Likewise, the Long data type is now 8 bytes, instead of its 4 bytes in VB 6.

 VB 6 Tip: The venerable VB 6 Variant data type in VB 6 is no longer supported in VB 2005; you should use the Object type instead. Object and the types that derive from it are discussed at greater length in Chapter 3.

Intrinsic and User-Defined Types

VB 6 and VB 2005 support two types of intrinsic data types and user-defined types. *Intrinsic* data types are those types that are built into the language. Examples of intrinsic data types are Integer, Short, and Char. *User-defined types* (UDT), on the other hand, are data types defined by programmers. Examples of user-defined data types are classes and structures. Most of the data types discussed in this chapter are intrinsic data types; Chapter 3 will discuss user-defined data types in more detail.

Table 2-1. Data types in VB 2005

VB 2005 type	Size (bytes)	VB 6 type (size in bytes)
Boolean	Depends on implementing platform	Boolean
Byte	1	Byte
Char	2	N/A
Date	8	Date
Decimal	16	Currency (8), Decimal (12)
Double	8	Double
Integer	4	Integer (2)
Long	8	Long (4)
Object	4	Variant
SByte	1	N/A
Short	2	N/A
Single	4	Single
String (variable size only)	Depends	String (supports fixed and variable size)
UInteger	4	N/A
ULong	8	N/A
UShort	2	N/A
User-Defined (Structure)	Depends	User-Defined (Type)

In both VB 6 and VB 2005, data types fall into one of two categories based on how they are stored and accessed:

Value types

A value type holds its data within its own memory allocation. You can access a value type directly without having to create a reference to it. Examples of value types are Integer and Single.

Reference types

A reference type contains a pointer to another memory location that holds the data. Examples of reference types are String and Object. We will discuss reference types in more detail in Chapter 3.

Variables in an application are stored in one of two different locations in memory: either on the stack or on the heap. *Stacks* are used for storing variables created in a function and are destroyed when the function exits. A *heap*, on the other hand, is used to store long-lived variables such as global and static variables.

Value types are stored directly on the stack at execution time, as opposed to being stored on the heap, as is done for reference types. You can access a value type directly without needing to create a reference to it. For a reference type, you must use a variable that contains a reference to the value of the type.

Variables

In VB 2005, you declare a variable with the Dim (dimension) keyword and you specify its type using the As keyword:

```
Dim num1
Dim num2 As Integer
```

The first statement declares num1, by default, to be an Object type. The Object type is the base class of all the classes in the .NET Framework. You can think of the Object type as equivalent to the Variant type in VB 6.

The second statement explicitly declares num2 to be an Integer variable.

The following statements declare num1 as a Short type and then assign a value to it:

```
'---range: -32768 <--> 32767
Dim num1 As Short
num1 = 32767
```

You should always specify the data type of a variable, because this assures the variable is *strongly typed*. Strong typing reduces the likelihood of runtime errors and makes your application much more efficient.

In VB 2005, to ensure that variables are declared with a data type (strongly typed), you should add the Option Strict On statement at the top of your code file. All variables must now be declared with a type.

You'll learn more about the importance of strong typing, also known as *early binding*, in Chapter 3.

In VB 2005, you must declare all of the variables that you use, although you can work around this restriction and use variables without first declaring them with the Option Explicit Off statement. VB 2005 turns on Option Explicit On by default.

 VB 6 Tip: VB 6 turns on Option Explicit Off by default. In both VB 6 and VB 2005, it is advisable for you to turn Option Explicit on, because using variables without first declaring them can easily inject potential bugs into your program.

Scope of Variables

The scope of a variable determines which parts of a program can access it. Consider the following VB 6 code:

```
For i = 0 To 10
    Dim j As Integer
    ...

Next i
j = 0 '<-- j is still accessible
```

Notice that the variable j was declared within the For loop. Outside the loop, j is still accessible.

In VB 2005, accessing a variable outside the scope in which it was declared is not allowed. Hence trying to access j outside the For loop will result in a compile-time error.

As shown in Figure 2-1, when you assign the value of one value type to another (num2 = num1), VB 2005—or more correctly, .NET—makes a copy of the value type:

```
Dim num1 as Short
Dim num2 as Short
num1 = -32768
num2 = num1
```

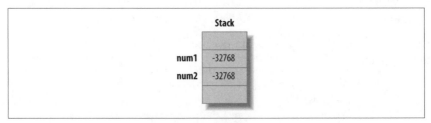

Figure 2-1. Representation of a value type in memory

Contrast this to the reference type. When you assign the value of a reference type to another, it causes the second variable to make a reference to the first without creating another copy of the value. The following example assigns one string variable to another:

```
Dim str1, str2 As String
str1 = "VB"
str2 = str1
```

The memory allocation of str1 and str2 is as shown in the Figure 2-2.

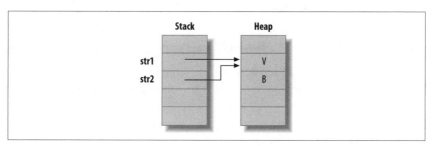

Figure 2-2. Representation of a reference type in memory

Unlike VB 6, with VB 2005, you can declare two variables to be of the same type in a single statement, as follows:

```
Dim num1, num2 As Short
```

 VB 6 Tip: In VB 6, if you declare two variables in the same statement, as in the following Dim statement, the results are not the same:

```
Dim num1, num2 As Short
```

Here, num1 is of the Variant type and num2 is of the Short type.

In VB 2005, you can also declare two variables of different data types in the same statement:

```
Dim num1 As Short, num2, num3 As Integer
```

In this case, num1 is declared as Short, and num2 and num3 are both of type Integer.

Unlike VB 6, in VB 2005, you can declare and initialize a variable in the same statement:

```
Dim num1 As Short = 56
```

VB 2005 now supports three new unsigned data types: UShort, UInteger, and ULong.

In VB.NET 2002 and 2003, you can use the .NET Framework's unsigned types, but you cannot perform mathematical operations on them. With the new unsigned data type support in the new VB 2005, you can now do so.

The following statements declare unum as an unsigned 16-bit integer:

```
Dim unum As UShort
unum = 65535
```

Type Characters

Instead of using the As keyword to specify the data type of a variable, you can append one the following *type characters* to the end of the variable name instead:

- Integer: %
- Long: &
- Decimal: @
- Single: !
- Double: #
- String: $

For example, the following statement declares num to be an Integer type:

```
Dim num%
num = 5
```

While type characters in VB 2005 preserve a popular feature found in VB 6, many .NET developers feel they should be avoided and that spelling out the type name makes for code that is easier to maintain and read.

Constants

While variables are a powerful tool, there are times when you want their values to remain constant. Perhaps your program makes repeated use of the value of *pi* or the natural logarithm *e*. A *constant* is like a variable in that it can store a value; unlike a variable, the value of a constant cannot be changed while the program runs. You declare constants using the Const keyword. The following definition assigns the value 3.14 to a constant whose name is pi and then uses it in calculating the area of a circle:

```
Const pi As Double = 3.14
Dim radius as Double = 5
Dim area as Double = pi * radius ^ 2
```

A constant of this type is sometimes called a *symbolic constant*, because it uses a word to represent a value. VB 2005 supports two additional kinds of constants: literals (see "Literals") and enumerations, or enums (See "Enumerations").

Literals

As in VB 6, a *literal*, or *literal constant*, as it is sometimes called, represents a particular value in text. For example, the number 32, as it appears in this sentence, is a literal constant. The value of 32 is always 32. Likewise, a quoted string like "Hello World" is also a literal constant. Literal types include Booleans, integers, floating-point numbers, strings, characters, and dates. Any number that is within the range of Integer types, such as 32, is an Integer type by default.

For example, the following statements assign the literal A to ch1 and ch2, both of which are Char types:

```
'---assign the character "A" to ch1 and ch2
Dim ch1 As Char = "A"c
Dim ch2 As Char = Chr(65)
Dim longValue as Long = 100L
```

To represent the quotation character (") in a string variable, use the quotation character twice in succession, as in the following snippet:

```
Dim str As String
' assigns str to "He said: "VB is so cool!""
str = "He said: ""VB is so cool!"""
```

To assign a date and time to a DateTime variable, use the # character:

```
Dim timeNow As DateTime
timeNow = #3/22/2005 10:01:19 AM#
```

To represent a large number, you can use the exponent symbol (E) to separate its mantissa (the significant digits; 3.8896, in the example below) and its exponent (a power of 10; 23, in this case):

```
Dim f As Double
f = 3.8896E+23
```

Enumerations

Sometimes it is easier to work with named constants than with numeric constants. *Enumerations* provide a powerful tool for creating logically related collections of named constants, such as the names of the primary colors, or the days of the week. For example, you might wish to represent the days of the week with numbers, such as 1 for Monday, 2 for Tuesday, and so on.

But when it comes to writing a program, it will likely be more intuitive to use the names of the days instead. You can do so by declaring an enumeration that associates each day of the week with a number.

 VB 6 Tip: Enumerations are not new in VB 2005; VB 6 programmers should already be familiar with enumerations.

The following shows the Week enumeration:

```
Enum Week
    Sunday = 0
    Monday = 1
    Tuesday = 2
    Wednesday = 3
    Thursday = 4
    Friday = 5
    Saturday = 6
End Enum
```

To use the enumeration, declare a variable of type Week:

```
Dim theWeek As Week
```

You can now assign the day of a week using a named constant:

```
theWeek = Week.Monday   ' or
theWeek = 1             ' both are equivalent
```

 Note that if you turn Option Strict On, the second statement above should be:

```
theWeek = CType(1, Week)
```

You need to explicitly convert the Integer value to the enumeration. In "Type Conversion," later in this chapter, you will learn about the Option Strict statement in more detail.

If you do not explicitly perform the conversion, Visual Studio 2005 will underline the number 1. You can position your cursor under the number and click on the down arrow (see Figure 2-3). Visual Studio 2005 will suggest to you the remedy. This feature is known as AutoCorrect.

To print out the month, you can use either of the following:

```
MsgBox(theWeek)            ' prints out 1
MsgBox(theWeek.ToString) ' prints out Monday
```

Besides defining your own enumerations, there are also predefined enumerations with which you might already be familiar. For example, the result from the MsgBox function is an enumeration called MsgBoxResult:

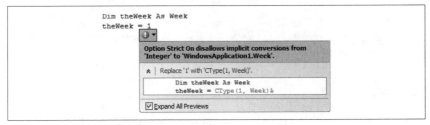

Figure 2-3. AutoCorrect in Visual Studio 2005

```
Dim response As MsgBoxResult
response = MsgBox("Are you sure?", MsgBoxStyle.YesNo)
If response = MsgBoxResult.Yes Then
    ' do something
Else
    ' do something
End If
```

Strings

As in VB 6, VB 2005 String types are used to represent text and are a good example of a reference type, as you saw in "Variables," earlier in this chapter. Strings in .NET are immutable, which means that once you've assigned a value to a string variable, it cannot be changed. If the value of a string variable is changed, another string object is created during runtime. Consider this example:

```
Dim st As String
st = "Hello"
st &= " World!"
MsgBox(st)  ' prints "Hello World!"
```

In the above example, two string objects are involved: one for the initialization and one for the concatenation. This problem gets worse if you are doing concatenation in a loop, like the following:

```
Dim i As Integer, str As String = ""
For i = 0 To 10000
    str &= i.ToString
Next
```

A much more efficient way to manipulate strings is to use the StringBuilder class, located in the System.Text namespace:

```
Dim i As Integer, str As New _
    System.Text.StringBuilder()
For i = 0 To 10000
    str.Append(i.ToString)
Next
```

The "_" (underscore) character is the continuation character in Visual Basic (all versions). It is used to break a long statement into multiple lines.

Arrays

As in VB 6, a VB 2005 *array* is a collection of variables in which each variable is identified by an index, like mailboxes on a street or players on a team.

For example, the following declaration defines num1 as an array by adding open and closed parentheses to its name:

```
Dim num1() As Integer
```

Note that this declaration simply declares num1 to be an array; the actual size of the array is not known yet. To get num1 to point to an actual array, use the New keyword:

```
num1 = New Integer() {1, 2, 3}
```

num1 is now an array containing three members of Integer data type with values 1, 2, and 3.

Here are some other possible ways to declare and initialize an array:

```
Dim num2(2) As Integer
num2(0) = 1
num2(1) = 2
num2(2) = 3
```

The size of the array is one plus the number declared, as is the case in VB 6. In the above case, the valid index is from 0 to 2, giving a total of 3 members. Note that the following is not allowed:

```
Dim num2(2) As Integer = New Integer
'---Not allowed since size is
'    already indicated
```

You can also combine the declaration together with the initialization:

```
Dim num3() As Integer = _
    New Integer() {1, 2, 3}
```

The following are not allowed:

```
Dim num3() As Integer = New Integer()
'---Not allowed; missing {}

Dim num3() As Integer = New Integer(3)
'---Not allowed; missing {}
```

```
Dim num3( ) As New Integer
'---Not allowed, arrays cannot use New

Dim num3() as New Integer( ) {1,2,3}
'---Syntax error
```

Once an array is declared, you can change its size by using the ReDim keyword:

```
Dim num4() As Integer() = New Integer() {1, 2, 3}
ReDim num4(5)
```

 VB 6 Tip: In VB 6, you can only ReDim an array if the array is initially declared as a variable length array, as the following shows:

```
' array is fixed length
Dim num1(3) As Integer
ReDim num1(5) '---error

' array is variable length
Dim num2( ) As Integer
ReDim num2(5) '---OK
```

When an array is redimensioned, all its previous values will be lost. To retain the previous values, use the Preserve keyword:

```
ReDim Preserve num4(5)
```

VB 2005 adds the new To keyword. You can explicitly specify the range of an array using the To keyword:

```
Dim num1(0 To 19) As Integer
```

 Note that the To keyword is used only to make your code more readable; you cannot alter the lower bounds of the array to, say, 1. The only bound must be 0.

Note that in VB 6, you can change the base of an array using the Option Base statement. However, VB 2005 does not allow you to change the base of an array.

Type Conversion

You perform a *type conversion* when you need to convert or assign values from one type to another. This is also known in some circles as *casting*. Consider the following code:

```
Dim num1 as Short = 25
Dim num2 as Long
num2 = num1
```

In this case, the VB 2005 compiler will automatically perform an *implicit* conversion from the Short type to the Long type. Since all the values that could be stored by the Short type can fit into a Long type, this conversion is known as a *widening conversion* and is a safe operation. The reverse of widening is a *narrowing conversion*, which is a conversion from a data type that has a larger range to one with a lower range. Consider the following:

```
Dim num1 As Long = 25
Dim num2 As Short
num2 = num1
```

In this example, num1 may potentially contain a value that will cause an overflow in num2 if the assignment takes place. In VB 2005, you can restrict automatic data type conversion by using the Option Strict statement. By default, in VB 2005, the Option Strict statement is set to Off.

> **VB 6 Tip**: In VB 6, there is no Option Strict statement. Hence, the design decision of VB 2005 was to turn Option Strict Off by default so that VB 6 code can be migrated easily.

If you turn Option Strict On, you will need to perform an *explicit* conversion (or else the compiler will complain):

```
'---if option strict on
num2 = CShort(num1)
'--OR--
num2 = CType(num1, Short)
```

> You should preferably turn Option Strict On, so that any narrowing operations you are doing are flagged. This will allow you to take action to catch potential errors that might result from a narrowing conversion. Note that in VB 6, performing a narrowing conversion will not set off a warning since the Option Strict statement is not supported.
>
> **VB 6 Tip**: The familiar type conversion functions like CInt, CStr, and CSng in VB 6 are still supported in VB 2005. In addition, VB 2005 supports the general purpose CType function, which allows you to specify the data type to convert to.

When performing a narrowing conversion, you should always take care to ensure that the operation will not result in a runtime error, such as performing the operation within a Try-Catch block. See "Error-Handling," later in this chapter, for more details.

Operators

VB 2005 supports the various operators shown in Table 2-2.

Table 2-2. Operators supported in VB 2005

Type	Language element	Description
Arithmetic	^	Raises to the power of
	–	Subtraction
	*	Multiplication
	/	Division
	\	Integer Division
	Mod	Modulus (remainder)
	+	Addition
Assignment	=	Assigns a value to a variable or property
	^=	Raises the value of a variable to the power of an expression and assigns the result back to the variable (new in VB 2005)
	*=	Multiplies the value of a variable by the value of an expression and assigns the result to the variable (new in VB 2005)
	/=	Divides the value of a variable by the value of an expression and assigns the result to the variable (new in VB 2005)
	\=	Divides the value of a variable by the value of an expression and assigns the integer result to the variable (new in VB 2005)
	+=	Adds the value of an expression to the value of a variable and assigns the result to the variable (works for strings as well) (new in VB 2005)
	-=	Subtracts the value of an expression from the value of a variable and assigns the result to the variable (new in VB 2005)
	&=	Concatenates a String expression to a String variable and assigns the result to the variable (new in VB 2005)
Comparison	=	Equal
	<>	Not equal to
	<	Less than
	>	Greater than
	<=	Less than or equal to
	>=	Greater than or equal to
	Like	Compares a string against a pattern
	Is	Compares two object reference variables
	IsNot	Compares two object reference variables
Concatenation	&	Concatenates two strings
	+	Concatenates two strings

Table 2-2. Operators supported in VB 2005 (continued)

Type	Language element	Description
Logical/bitwise operations	Not	Logical negation on a Boolean expression
	And	Logical conjunction on two Boolean expressions, or bitwise conjunction on two numeric expressions
	Or	Logical disjunction on two Boolean expressions, or bitwise disjunction on two numeric values
	Xor	Logical exclusion operation on two Boolean expressions, or bitwise exclusion on two numeric expressions
	AndAlso	Short-circuiting logical conjunction on two expressions (new in VB 2005)
	OrElse	Short-circuiting logical disjunction on two expressions (new in VB 2005)
Miscellaneous operations	AddressOf	Creates a procedure delegate instance that references the specific procedure (new in VB 2005)
	GetType	Returns a Type object for the specified type (new in VB 2005)

When testing for the equality of numeric values, use the = operator. Use the Is operator to test the equality of objects. Chapter 3 will discuss the use of the Is operator in greater detail.

 VB 6 Tip: Of particular interest to VB 6 users is the new support for assignment operators in Visual Basic 2005. In VB 6, to increment a variable, you must write code that looks something like this:

```
var = var + 1
```

In Visual Basic 2005, you can now rewrite the line as:

```
var += 1
```

The IsNot operator is new in VB 2005. Often you need to negate the comparison of an object, such as:

```
Dim obj As Button
If Not obj Is Nothing Then
    ' obj contains an object reference
    ....
End If
```

In this case, your code will be more readable if you use the IsNot operator:

```
If obj IsNot Nothing Then
    ' obj contains an object reference
    ....
End If
```

Statements

As in VB 6, a complete program instruction in VB 2005 is called a *statement*. Programs consist of sequences of statements. You end each statement with a carriage return.

In VB 2005, spaces, tabs, and carriage returns (newlines) are considered to be "whitespace." Extra whitespace is ignored in VB 2005, as in VB 6, a feature that many consider an endearing (and forgiving) quality of the language.

Decision-Making (Branching) Statements

VB 2005 retains the traditional VB 6 statements for decision making but adds a few new wrinkles of its own. Decision-making statements fall into two categories:

- If-Then-Else
- Select-Case

If-Then-Else

Just as in VB 6, in VB 2005, you make decisions using the If-Then-Else construct.

```
If <condition> Then
    <statement(s)>
Else
    <statement(s)>
End if
```

Here is a short example:

```
Dim day As Short = 4
Dim dayofWeek As String
If day = 1 Then
    dayofWeek = "Monday"
End If
```

In the preceding code, if day is equal to 1, the string "Monday" is then assigned to the dayofWeek variable. For a one-line statement, you can shorten the above code to:

```
If day = 1 Then dayofWeek = "Monday"
```

However, if you have multiple statements to execute if a condition is met, use of the End If statement is mandatory. VB 2005 lets you pack a block of conditional code into a single line. For example, the following block of code:

```
If day = 1 Then
    dayofWeek = "Monday"
    currentTime = Now
End If
```

is equivalent to this single line of code:

```
If day = 1 Then dayofWeek = "Monday" : currentTime = Now
```

The grouping of several statements into a single line using the : character, as shown in the preceding snippet, is useful in cases where you want to group multiple statements into a single line to improve the readability of your code. The grouping feature is also useful for organizing a related group of variables.

You can also nest several If-Then-Else statements, as shown in Example 2-1.

Example 2-1. Nesting If-Then-Else statements

```
Dim day As Short = 4
Dim dayofWeek As String

If day = 1 Then
    dayofWeek = "Monday"
Else
    If day = 2 Then
        dayofWeek = "Tuesday"
    Else
        If day = 3 Then
            dayofWeek = "Wednesday"
        Else
            If day = 4 Then
                dayofWeek = "Thursday"
            Else
                If day = 5 Then
                    dayofWeek = "Friday"
                Else
                    If day = 6 Then
                        dayofWeek = "Saturday"
                    Else
                        If day = 0 Then
                            dayofWeek = "Sunday"
                        Else
                            Msgbox("Number out of range")
                        End If
                    End If
                End If
            End If
```

Example 2-1. Nesting If-Then-Else statements (continued)

```
        End If
    End If
End If
```

Note the matching End If statement for each If statement. If you have multiple nested If-Then-Else constructs, you can simplify the above code using the ElseIf keyword (also supported in VB 6), as shown in Example 2-2.

Example 2-2. Using the ElseIf keyword

```
If day = 1 Then
    dayofWeek = "Monday"
ElseIf day = 2 Then
    dayofWeek = "Tuesday"
ElseIf day = 3 Then
    dayofWeek = "Wednesday"
ElseIf day = 4 Then
    dayofWeek = "Thursday"
ElseIf day = 5 Then
    dayofWeek = "Friday"
ElseIf day = 6 Then
    dayofWeek = "Saturday"
ElseIf day = 0 Then
    dayofWeek = "Sunday"
Else
    MsgBox("Number out of range")
End If
```

Note that if you use the ElseIf keyword, the number of End If statements is reduced to one (in this example).

Short-Circuiting

Short-circuiting is a compiler optimization technique that reduces the checking of redundant conditions in a decision-making statement. In both the logical And and Or operations, both conditions are evaluated regardless of their results. To short-circuit the And operation, you can replace it with the new AndAlso operator so that if the first condition is false, the second condition is not evaluated.

Likewise, to short-circuit the Or operations, you can use the OrElse operator. If the first condition evaluates to true, the second condition is not evaluated.

VB 6 does not support short-circuiting when evaluating an expression. Hence, in order not to break existing code, Microsoft added the AndAlso and OrElse operators in VB 2005 for short-circuiting.

Select...Case

If you have multiple conditions to test, it is often much easier (and more readable) to use the Select...Case construct. Example 2-3 shows a rewrite of the previous code segment using the Select...Case construct.

Example 2-3. Using the Select...Case statement

```
Select Case day
    Case 1 : dayofWeek = "Monday"
    Case 2 : dayofWeek = "Tuesday"
    Case 3 : dayofWeek = "Wednesday"
    Case 4 : dayofWeek = "Thursday"
    Case 5 : dayofWeek = "Friday"
    Case 6 : dayofWeek = "Saturday"
    Case 0 : dayofWeek = "Sunday"
    Case Else : Msgbox( _
        "Number out of range")
End Select
```

Looping (Iteration) Statements

VB 2005 provides several looping constructs. They are all supported in VB 6 as well, unless otherwise noted:

```
For
For-Each
While
Do-While
Do-Until
```

Each of the following examples (Example 2-4 through Example 2-8) prints a series of array members with indexes ranging from 0 to 5 using one of the looping constructs supported by VB 2005.

Example 2-4. Using the For loop

```
Dim num( ) As Integer = {1, 2, 3, 4, 5, 6}
For n as Integer = 0 To 5
    Console.Write(num(n))
Next
```

> **VB 6 Tip:** In VB 6, you need to declare the loop variant (n) in a separate statement. Only VB 2005 allows you to declare it and use it at the same time.

Example 2-5. Using the For-Each loop

```
Dim num( ) As Integer = {1, 2, 3, 4, 5, 6}
For Each i As Integer In num
    Console.Write(i)
Next
```

Example 2-6. Using the While loop

```
Dim num( ) As Integer = {1, 2, 3, 4, 5, 6}
Dim j As Integer = 0
While j <= 5
    Console.Write(num(j))
    j += 1
End While
```

 VB 6 Tip: In VB 6, you use the While-Wend statement to implement a While loop.

Example 2-7. Using the Do-While loop

```
Dim num( ) As Integer = {1, 2, 3, 4, 5, 6}
Dim k As Integer = 0
Do While k <= 5
    Console.Write(num(k))
    k += 1
Loop
```

Example 2-8. Using the Do-Until loop

```
Dim num( ) As Integer = {1, 2, 3, 4, 5, 6}
Dim m As Integer = 0
Do
    Console.Write(num(m))
    m += 1
Loop Until m > 5
```

Functions and Subroutines

VB 2005 supports both functions and subroutines. Basically, support for functions and subroutines is the same in VB 2005 as it is in VB 6. However, VB 2005 provides you with an additional way to return values in a function by means of the new Return statement. VB 2005 programmers have three choices: they can write their own functions, continue using most of the VB 6 functions they have come to know and love, or tap into the rich functionality of the .NET Framework Class Library through the new My namespace (see "My Namespace," later in this chapter).

Exiting or Skipping a Loop

You can exit a loop at any time by using one of the following statements:

```
Exit For
Exit Do
Exit While
```

In VB 2005, you can transfer control immediately to the next iteration of a loop by using the Continue keyword. Consider the following:

```
For i As Integer = 0 To 10
    ' prints out all odd
    ' numbers from 0 to 10
    If i Mod 2 = 0 Then Continue For
    MsgBox(i)
Next
```

The preceding code snippet prints out all the odd numbers from 0 to 10. Note that the Continue keyword can also be used with a While loop and a Do-While loop.

Function

A *function* is a block of code that performs some operations and then returns a value. For example, the following function Area takes in two input parameters, computes the area, and then returns the result:

```
Public Function Area(ByVal length As Single, _
            ByVal breadth As Single) As Single
    Dim result As Single
    result = length * breadth
    Return result
End Function
```

To invoke a function, you simply call the function name with the required argument(s):

```
Dim areaOfRect As Single = Area(4, 5)
```

 VB 6 Tip: In VB 6, only functions require the mandatory use of parentheses around the parameter list. But in VB 2005, all functions or subroutine calls require parentheses around the parameter list (even if the parameter list is empty).

The value returned by the Area function is then assigned to the areaOfRect variable.

In VB 6, you use the function name to return the value of a function, like this:

```
Public Function Area(ByVal length As Single, _
          ByVal breadth As Single) As Single
    Dim result As Single
    result = length * breadth
    Area = result
End Function
```

In VB 2005, you can either use the Return keyword or the function name to return the value of a function. Note that when a Return statement is encountered in a function, the execution is immediately transferred back to the statement that called it.

Subroutine

A *subroutine* is similar to a function, except that it does not return a value. For example, the following subroutine PrintMessage accepts a single input parameter and prints a message box.

```
Public Sub PrintMessage(ByVal str As String)
    MsgBox(str)
End Sub
```

To invoke a subroutine, you simply call the subroutine name and pass it the required argument(s):

```
PrintMessage("File deletion completed.")
```

 VB 6 Tip: In VB 6, you can call the PrintMessage subroutine without using parentheses to enclose the parameter list:

```
PrintMessage "File deletion completed."
```

Passing Arguments

There are two ways to pass values to a subroutine or function:

- By value
- By reference

Let's take a closer look at these two methods in the following sections.

Passing by value

Consider the following subroutine:

```
Public Sub ProcessValue(ByVal num As Integer)
    num += 1
    MsgBox("In ProcessValue( ), num is " & num)
End Sub
```

The ProcessValue subroutine takes a single input parameter: num. The parameter declaration is preceded by the ByVal keyword.

By default, Visual Basic 2005 passes an argument via ByVal. In VB 6, the default is ByRef (see "Passing by reference," next).

The following statements call the ProcessValue subroutine and display a value at each stage:

```
Dim num As Integer = 5
MsgBox("Before ProcessValue( ), num is " & num)
ProcessValue(num)    ' pass by value
MsgBox("After ProcessValue( ), num is " & num)
```

You will realize that the value of num remains at 5 before and after calling the ProcessValue subroutine.

As you can deduce, even though the variable num is modified within the subroutine, the change is not reflected outside the subroutine. When you pass an argument by value, a copy of the variable is created to be used within the subroutine. When the subroutine exits, the variable is destroyed.

Passing by reference

Consider the following subroutine:

```
Public Sub ProcessValue(ByRef num As Integer)
    num += 1
    MsgBox("In ProcessValue( ), num is " & num)
End Sub
```

The ProcessValue subroutine takes in a single input parameter: num. The parameter declaration is preceded with the ByRef keyword.

The following statements call the ProcessValue subroutine and display the value at every stage:

```
Dim num As Integer = 5
MsgBox("Before ProcessValue( ), num is " & num)
ProcessValue(num)    ' pass by value
MsgBox("After ProcessValue( ), num is " & num)
```

In contrast to passing by value, when you pass an argument by reference, the subroutine receives a reference that points to the location where the argument is stored in memory. When the variable is modified within the subroutine, the change will affect the original variable. Hence, the change remains even after the subroutine exits.

Optional parameters

Consider the following definition of a modified `PrintMessage` subroutine:

```
Public Sub PrintMessage(ByVal str1 As String, _
                        ByVal str2 As String, _
        Optional ByVal str3 As String = "rocks!")
    MsgBox(str1 & str2 & str3)
End Sub
```

This version of the `PrintMessage` subroutine takes three input parameters: `str1`, `str2`, and `str3`. The first two are required; `str3` is an optional parameter, as called out by the `Optional` keyword. For an optional parameter, a default value is required.

Optional arguments must always be declared last in a subroutine definition. You can specify one or more optional parameters.

 VB 6 Tip: In VB 6, optional parameters are not required to have default values, but in VB 2005, optional parameters must have default values.

When you call the subroutine, you pass the arguments in the order specified by the parameter list. The following subroutine calls `PrintMessage`, passes the strings "Visual" and "Basic" as arguments, using the optional arguments in one case but not in the others:

```
'--- with and without optional arguments

' prints out Visual Basic rocks!
PrintMessage("Visual ", "Basic ")

' prints out Visual Basic rocks!
PrintMessage("Visual ", "Basic ", )

' prints out Visual Basic really rocks!
PrintMessage("Visual ", "Basic ", "really rocks!")
```

You can also leave out the optional argument by using a comma (,).

Error Handling

There are two main types of coding errors that programmers generally have to deal with:

- Compile-time errors
- Runtime errors

In VB 2005, the background compiler kicks into action every time you type in a line of code. It dynamically compiles your code and warns you of errors before you actually compile it.

In the former case, the compiler detects a syntax error and the IDE handles the error and calls it to the attention of the programmer so that immediate action can be taken to fix the problem. Runtime errors occur while an application is running. It is this type of error that must (and can) be prevented.

To ensure that an application is as robust and bug free as possible, it is important to anticipate as best you can all of the errors that might occur while your program is running. In VB 2005, error handling has been much improved over VB 6. VB 2005 now supports both structured and unstructured error handling.

VB 6 Tip: In VB 6, error handling was unstructured, performed using the primitive On Error and On Error Resume Next statements. The specific information about an error that occurred can be retrieved from the Err object.

Try-Catch-Finally

In VB 2005, you can implement structured error handling using the Try...Catch...Finally construct. Basically, you place any code that could possibly trigger a runtime error, such as a disk access, into a Try block. Any errors that happen within the Try block will be caught and serviced by the Catch block(s) that follow. This is where you can take actions to correct the error or clean up any resources that you've allocated. The Finally block is executed whether an error occur in the Try block or not. The Finally block is a good place to perform housekeeping chores such as closing a database or file connection.

Example 2-9 shows how you can use Try...Catch...Finally statements to catch errors at multiple levels within a procedure that performs an integer division of two numbers. Note the use of multiple Catch blocks to handle exceptions that range from the specific (InvalidCastException and DivideByZeroException) to the most general (Exception).

Example 2-9. Using Try...Catch...Finally statements to handle runtime errors

```
'===Error Handling===
Dim num1, num2, result As Integer
Try
    num1 = InputBox("Please enter num1")
    num2 = InputBox("Please enter num2")
```

Example 2-9. Using Try...Catch...Finally statements to handle runtime errors (continued)

```
    result = num1 \ num2
    MsgBox(result)
Catch invalidCast As InvalidCastException
    MsgBox("Please enter numbers only")
Catch divisionByZero As DivideByZeroException
    MsgBox("Division by zero error")
Catch ex As Exception
    MsgBox(ex.ToString)
Finally
    MsgBox("This line is always printed.")
End Try
```

When the user enters a non-numeric input for one of the numbers, the InvalidCastException exception will be raised and the message "Please enter numbers only" will be printed. If the user enters a 0 for num2, it results in a division by zero error and raises the DivideByZeroException exception. The Exception exception is the root of all exceptions and will catch any exceptions not caught by the earlier Catch statements. The statement within the Finally block is always executed, regardless of whether any exception has been raised.

Throwing Exceptions

Besides catching errors using the Try...Catch...Finally construct and the predefined exceptions available in the .NET Class Library, you can also throw your own custom exceptions by using the Throw keyword. The Throw keyword allows you to throw an exception so that you can handle the exception with the structured exception-handling code.

Consider the following example:

```
Public Function divide(ByVal num1 As Single, _
                       ByVal num2 As Single) _
                       As Single
    If num2 = 0 Then Throw New _
        Exception("num2 cannot be zero!")
    Return num1 / num2
End Function
```

In this divide function, if num2 is zero, you will throw your own exception (using the Exception class) with your own custom error message.

A user of this function can then catch the error like this:

```
Try
    MsgBox(divide(4, 0))
Catch ex As Exception
    MsgBox(ex.ToString)
End Try
```

The variable ex will contain detailed information of the exception when it occurs. To display the error message, simply use the ToString method.

My Namespace

One of the problems faced by VB 6 programmers moving to VB 2005 is figuring out which class in the .NET Framework is the appropriate class to use to solve a particular problem. To simplify the transition, VB 2005 provides the new My namespace, which encapsulates some of the most common functionalities that developers need in their daily work.

 VB 6 Tip: Most VB 6 predefined functions are still supported in VB 2005. They are located within the Microsoft. VisualBasic namespace (which is automatically referenced by default in all VB 2005 projects) and so you can continue to use your favorite VB 6 functions without doing anything extra.

The My namespace exposes several areas of functionality, as shown in the IntelliSense pop-up in Figure 2-4.

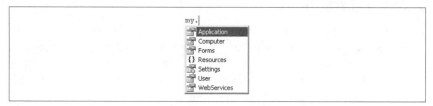

Figure 2-4. The objects exposed by the My namespace

The aim of the My namespace is to provide direct access to commonly used libraries (in the .NET Framework) like Resources that were previously difficult to access. The intuitive hierarchy of the My namespace provides a mechanism that VB 2005 developers can use to easily navigate the .NET Framework class libraries and locate the classes required to perform a particular task. For example, suppose you want to play an audio file in your application. Which class should you use? Using the My namespace, it is easy to locate the right class to use. As it turns out, the class to use can be found in My.Computer.Audio.Play!

The objects exposed by the My namespace are:

My.Application
    Provides properties, methods, and events related to the current application.

`My.Computer`

Provides properties for manipulating computer components, such as audio, the clock, the keyboard, the filesystem, and so on.

`My.User`

Provides access to the current user's security context. For Windows applications, the access is read-write, while access for web applications is read-only.

`My.Forms`

Provides properties for accessing an instance of each Windows Form declared in the current project.

`My.Settings`

Provides properties and methods for accessing the application's settings.

`My.Webservices`

Provides properties for creating and accessing a single instance of each XML web service referenced by the current project.

> The `My` namespace is not just a static shortcut to the class libraries in the .NET Framework. Depending on your project type, the `My.Forms`, `My.Resources`, `My.Settings`, and `My.Webservices` objects will dynamically display the relevant objects and classes.

Here are some examples of how to use the `My` namespace. You can use the `My.Application` object to discover the installation path of the current application:

```
Dim appPath As String = _
    My.Application.Info.DirectoryPath
```

You can use the `My.Computer` object determine whether a file exists. At the same time, you can also play a system audio sound:

```
Dim exists As Boolean
exists = _
    My.Computer.FileSystem.FileExists( _
    "c:\file.txt")
If Not exists Then
    My.Computer.Audio.PlaySystemSound( _
        System.Media.SystemSounds.Exclamation)
    MsgBox("File does not exist")
End If
```

You can also play a specific audio file:

```
My.Computer.Audio.Play( _
    "C:\WINDOWS\Media\chimes.wav")
```

File management is one of the most common tasks that developers need to perform. Using the My.Computer.FileSystem object, you can access all the various file handling routines in one place (see Figure 2-5).

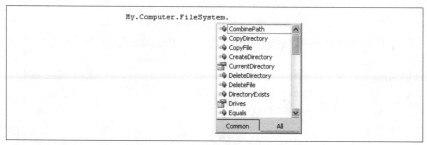

Figure 2-5. The routines in the My.Computer.FileSystem object

Another useful object that resides in My.Computer is the Network object. With it, you can perform a task such as downloading a file from the network and saving it locally. The following example downloads a *.gif* file from a web site and saves to your local *C:* drive.

```
My.Computer.Network.DownloadFile( _
    "http://www.oreilly.com/catalog/" & _
    "covers/aspnetadn.s.gif", _
    "c:\images\0596008120.jpg")
```

In a Windows application, you can access the collections of forms in your application and their properties with the My.Forms object. For example, the following statements set the Opacity property of a form to 50%:

```
My.Forms.Form1.Opacity = 0.5
' ---equivalent to---
Form1.Opacity = 0.5
```

If you have multiple web services references in a project, you can find them all in the My.WebServices object. For example, suppose you have added a web reference to the Translate web service in your application (see Figure 2-6) at *http://www.webservicex.net/TranslateService.asmx?WSDL*. The following example shows how to invoke the TranslateService web service through the My.WebServices object:

```
MsgBox(My.WebServices.TranslateService.Translate( _
    net.webservicex.www.Language.EnglishTOFrench, "Hello"))
```

In a web application, you can use My.User to determine whether a user is authenticated:

```
Response.Write(My.User.IsAuthenticated)
```

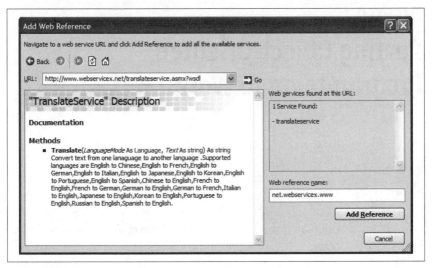

Figure 2-6. Adding a web reference

Summary

In this chapter, you have been taken on a whirlwind tour of VB 2005 syntax and seen how it compares with that of VB 6. If you are a VB 6 programmer, you'll be happy to have discovered that much of what you already know is still supported (or enhanced) in VB 2005. The new My namespace is another productive feature that Microsoft has built into the language.

In the next chapter, you will learn how you can use the object-oriented programming support found in VB 2005 to become even more productive than you already are, and you'll learn why object orientation is one of the most important additions to the Visual Basic language.

CHAPTER 3

Putting Object-Oriented Programming to Work

Not all object-oriented programming (OOP) concepts are new to Visual Basic. The language has had support for classes and interface-based programming since Version 4, and, arguably, the drag-and-drop controls that have been central to the Visual Basic programming paradigm since Version 1 are a sterling example of what reusable objects can achieve. When you drop a Button control onto a VB 6 form, for example, you create a new instance of the control in a way that is analogous to the way a class is instantiated in a traditional object-oriented language. Likewise, when you set the Caption property of a Button or call the Show method of a form, you perform tasks that are analogous to setting a property or calling a method on an object.

Still, it's hard to argue that VB 6 is a truly object-oriented language. It lacks support for such crucial features such as inheritance, which allows one class to derive its properties and functionality from another. Were that functionality present, for example, you would be able to create your own custom Buttons by deriving from the Button control that ships with VB 6. Interface-based programming is so difficult in VB 6 that few programmers have bothered to master it. VB 6 has no support for defining or working with interfaces, for example, and VB 6 programmers schooled in OOP principles must resort to virtual base classes to achieve the same result.

In the end, many—perhaps most—Visual Basic programmers have concluded that OOP is arcane and impossibly difficult, and irrelevant to the development of the applications that VB 6 programmers implement every day.

Visual Basic 2005 changes everything, and in this chapter, I'll not only make the case that OOP is a tool that can turbo charge your productivity as a developer, but I'll also show you how VB 2005 now makes it easy to incorporate the best practices of OOP into your applications.

So, let the journey begin!

Working with Classes and Objects

The advantage of OOP is that it facilitates code reuse. When you drag-and-drop a Button control onto a form, you don't worry about how it works; that's been taken care of by the control's designer. In addition, you're free to use as many Button controls on your form as you need and to modify each as required by changing its caption, color, shape, and—through event handling—even behavior. You can think of OOP as a set of tools that brings the same reusability you've grown accustomed to with VB 6 controls to the code you write to power your applications.

To understand OOP, you need to know about classes and objects. A *class* is like a template; it defines the essential features of some thing. A good analogy to a class is your concept of a car. When you hear the word "car," you no doubt quickly think of a vehicle with wheels, gas and brake pedals, a steering wheel, and so on before you think of a specific make. An *object*, on the other hand, is an instance of a class. A BMW sitting on a lot is a specific make of a car and, although it shares certain key features with every other car in the world, it is, like an object, a unique version, or instance, of the more general car class. A BMW is related to the general notion of a car as an object is to its defining class.

A car, regardless of its make, can be counted on to have a variety of properties, such as a color, some number of doors, and seats that are made of leather or vinyl. A class also has *properties*, as you'll see shortly, and you can assign them values and also find out what values have been assigned (though restrictions do apply).

A car also has certain behaviors and "knows" (in the hands of an experienced driver) how to accelerate, turn left, turn right, decelerate, or come to a stop. Every car includes the controls you need to make it do your bidding, and you expect to find them in more or less the same place regardless of make. A class has behaviors as well. These are defined by its *methods*.

When you step on the brake pedal of your car, the braking system gets to work to slow the vehicle. As a driver, you don't need to understand the inner workings of the braking system; you just need to know where to find the brake pedal and when to step on it. Likewise, when you use a method in a class, you need not understand its inner workings. All you need to know is how to invoke it, and what you can expect it to do.

Using the .NET Classes

Unlike VB 6, VB 2005 gets much of its work done by calling on the hundreds of classes provided by the .NET Framework 2.0, rather than the predefined functions of the traditional Visual Basic runtime or older COM-based libraries such as ADO (both of which are still supported in VB 2005). Collectively, these classes are known as the *.NET Framework Class Library*, or FCL.

VB 6 Functions and the .NET Base Class Library

Because VB 2005 is a language designed to work with the .NET Framework, some changes to the language are necessary to maintain interoperability with the Common Language Runtime. You've already seen many of these in Chapter 2.

The Common Language Runtime (CLR) is the heart of the .NET Framework. The CLR manages code execution and provides application services such as security, memory management, and cross-language integration.

In VB 2005, the .NET Framework includes new libraries that provide equivalent functionality to many VB 6 keywords and functions (although these VB 6 functions are still available in VB 2005).

To see the list of changes to the VB 6 language and their equivalents in Visual Basic 2005, refer to the MSDN Help Topic "Programming Element Support Changes Summary."

To see how application development (such as Windows and web development) have changed in Visual Basic 2005, refer to MSDN Help Topic "Help for Visual Basic 6.0 Users."

The .NET Class Libraries are contained in multiple DLLs, known as *assemblies*, and loaded only when they're needed. This has the advantage of reducing the time it takes to load a managed application. Due to the large number of classes that ship with the .NET Framework, Microsoft has logically grouped them into *namespaces*. Namespaces are used to arrange classes in groups based on the functionality they provide. For example, the System namespace contains fundamental classes that define commonly used value and reference data types, events and event handlers, interfaces, attributes, and processing exceptions.

Here are some other useful namespaces in the .NET Framework:

System

The System namespace contains fundamental classes and base classes that define commonly used value and reference data types, events and event handlers, interfaces, attributes, and processing exceptions.

System.Collections

The System.Collections namespace contains interfaces and classes that define various collections of objects, such as lists, queues, bit arrays, hash tables, and dictionaries.

System.Windows.Forms

The System.Windows.Forms namespace contains classes for creating Windows-based applications that take full advantage of the rich user interface features available in the Microsoft Windows operating system.

System.Web.UI

The System.Web.UI namespace provides classes and interfaces that allow you to create ASP.NET server controls and pages that will appear in your web applications as user interface elements.

System.Data

The System.Data namespace consists mostly of the classes that constitute the ADO.NET architecture for data access. The ADO.NET architecture enables you to build components that efficiently manage data from multiple data sources.

When you create a Visual Basic project in Visual Studio 2005, the IDE ensures that references to the most commonly used base class library assemblies are added before you begin to write code. However, if you need to use a type that is in an assembly you've not already referenced, you will need to add the missing reference to your code. The Add Reference dialog box in Visual Studio allows you to add an assembly without having to write code.

A .NET Framework Class Library assembly may contain several namespaces. For example, the *System.Data.dll* assembly contains several namespaces for classes that perform data access. To use the relevant libraries in the assembly, you need to use the Imports keyword to import them for use in your application, such as:

```
Imports System.Data
Imports System.Data.SqlClient
Imports System.Data.OleDb
```

For example, if you want to create a SqlDataReader object that reads data from a Microsoft SQL server, you would need to import the System.Data. SqlClient namespace with an Imports statement at the top of your code.

Once you have correctly referenced the namespace, you can then reference a SqlDataReader object in your code like this:

```
Dim reader As SqlDataReader
```

Alternatively, you can use the SqlDataReader object by its fully qualified name, like this:

```
Dim reader As _
    System.Data.SqlClient.SqlDataReader
```

The first approach is the recommended one, as it makes your code much more readable.

Commonly Referenced DLLs

Depending on the type of project you create, Visual Studio automatically adds references to the DLLs you are most likely to need. For Windows applications, these include:

- *System.dll*
- *System.Deployment.dll*
- *System.Drawing.dll*
- *System.Windows.Forms.dll*
- *System.Data.dll*
- *System.Xml.dll*

For web applications, the following DLLs are referenced by default:

- *System.dll*
- *System.Web.dll*
- *System.Data.dll*
- *System.Xml.dll*
- *System.Drawing.dll*

Creating Objects

In the .NET world, applications are built with classes and objects, either your own or those provided by the .NET Framework. To fully use the power of VB 2005, you need to understand how to work with them.

Since it's available, let's use the Stack class provided in the System.Collections namespace of the .NET Framework to illustrate how you can get productive with OOP. You'll see how to define your own version later in this chapter (see "Defining a Class," later in this chapter).

What Is a Stack?

A *stack* is a data structure that works based on the last in, first out (LIFO) principle. This means that the last item put on the stack is the first item that can be taken off, like a physical stack of plates.

Stacks are used quite often in programming. They are used to store subroutine arguments and return addresses. Stacks are also commonly used to evaluate mathematical expressions.

Adding an item to a stack is known as a *push* operation and removing an item from a stack is known as a *pop* operation.

The .NET Framework includes a Stack class, which is located in the System. Collections namespace.

VB 6 Tip: VB 6 does not provide a ready-to-use Stack class.

To drive a car, you need a real one, whether it's your own or a BMW you take for a spin at your local dealership. Likewise, to use a Stack class, whether it's your own or the .NET version, you must *instantiate*—that is, create—an instance of the class. Instantiating a class is, you might say, a classic example of reuse. From a single design, you can create as many instances of a Stack as you need for your application, just as the designs embedded in an automobile manufacturing plant are used to build multiple versions of the same car. You'll learn about customizing classes later in this chapter.

There are several ways to instantiate a Stack object, so let's take a look at them.

You use the Dim keyword to declare that a variable—s1, in this case—is of type Stack, just as you did for normal VB variables and constants in Chapter 2.

```
Dim s1 As Stack
```

You use the New keyword to instantiate a Stack object (i.e., create an instance of the class):

```
s1 = New Stack
```

You can also declare and instantiate an object in a single statement. The following two statements, for example, are equivalent:

```
Dim s2 As New System.Collections.Stack
' or
Dim s2 As System.Collections.Stack = New System.Collections.Stack
```

The parentheses following the name of a class are optional. (I will not be using parentheses for the class names in the examples throughout this book.) The following two statements are the same:

```
Dim s1 As New System.Collections.Stack
Dim s1 As New System.Collections.Stack( )
```

VB 6 Tip: In VB 6, assigning an object to a variable requires the use of the Set keyword:

```
'---VB6---
Set obj = New Class1
```

This has confused VB 6 developers who are sometimes unsure of when to use the Set keyword.

With VB 2005, Microsoft has eliminated this confusion, since the Set keyword is no longer used for object assignment:

```
'---VB2005---
obj = New Class1
```

Note that if you precede the previous statement with the Set keyword, Visual Studio 2005 will automatically remove it.

To use the Stack object, you could push in some values via the Push method:

```
'---Push items into the stack---
s1.Push("Hello ")
s1.Push("Visual ")
s1.Push("Basic ")
s1.Push("2005")
```

Get a count of the number of items in the Stack object by using the Count property:

```
'---Get the item count in the stack---
Dim itemCount As Integer = s1.Count
```

You could also pop the items out of the Stack object by using the Pop method:

```
'---Pop the items out from the stack---
For i As Integer = 0 To s1.Count - 1
    MsgBox(s1.Pop( )) ' strings are printed in the
                      ' reverse order they were pushed
Next
```

Example 3-1 shows the complete code needed to use the Stack class.

Example 3-1. Using a Stack object

```
Dim s1 As New System.Collections.Stack
'---Push items into the stack---
s1.Push("Hello ")
s1.Push("Visual ")
s1.Push("Basic ")
s1.Push("2005")

'---Get the item count in the stack---
Dim itemCount As Integer = s1.Count

'---Pop the items out from the stack---
For i As Integer = 0 To s1.Count - 1
    MsgBox(s1.Pop()) ' strings are printed in the
                     ' reverse order they were pushed
Next
```

Comparing Objects

If you want to check to see whether two variables are referencing the same object, you need to use the Is operator (the = operator cannot be used), as demonstrated in Example 3-2.

Example 3-2. Comparing two objects

```
Dim s1, s2 As System.Collections.Stack
s1 = New System.Collections.Stack
s2 = New System.Collections.Stack

If s1 Is s2 Then
    MsgBox("objs are the same")
Else
    '---this will be printed---
    MsgBox("ojs are not the same")
End If

'---Assigning s2 to s1; essentially s1 and s2 will
'---now point to the same object
s1 = s2
If s1 Is s2 Then
    '---this will be printed---
    MsgBox("objs are the same")
Else
    MsgBox("objs are not the same")
End If
```

Note that the Is operator is used only for comparing object references (if they are all referencing the same object); it cannot be used to compare the values of objects.

Besides the Is operator, you can also use the Equals method (available on all .NET objects) to compare the equality of two objects (that is, if the two objects are pointing to the same reference), like this:

```
If s1.Equals(s2) Then
    MsgBox("objs are the same")
Else
    MsgBox("objs are not the same")
End If
    ...
```

Shared Methods

Typically, you need to create an instance of a class before you can invoke its methods, as you've seen in the preceding example. However, there are exceptions to this rule. As an example, consider the File class in the System.IO namespace. The File class contains methods for file manipulation, such as copying, deleting, writing, reading, etc. To use the File class, you don't need to create an instance of the class; you simply invoke its method directly:

```
'---copies a file---
System.IO.File.Copy("C:\File1.txt", "C:\File1.bak")
```

The methods in the File class are known as *static* methods, the general term used by most object oriented languages, or as *shared* methods, the term and keyword used by VB 2005. A shared method can be invoked without creating an instance of its class.

Reusing and Customizing Classes

The use of classes in OOP allows you to build an application from discrete components, each of which encapsulates the variables and methods needed to carry out specific tasks. But as powerful as classes are for designing and implementing applications, the ability to reuse and customize them is what makes support for OOP such a powerful tool in Visual Basic 2005.

In this section, you'll see how you can create your own classes by modifying those provided by the .NET Framework. The same principles can also be applied to class libraries that you or your teams develop. In addition, you'll learn about the new generic classes in Visual Basic 2005 that are designed from scratch to be flexible in the range of types they accept.

Using Inheritance

One of the fundamental concepts of OOP is inheritance. Inheritance facilitates code reuse and allows you to extend and use the code that you have already written. Simply put, *inheritance* is the ability to extend the functionality of classes, and is the basis of the several techniques we discuss in this section.

The beauty of inheritance is that you can define all the common logic you need in a single master class—typically called the *base* or *parent* class—and then use inheritance to extend its logic in a *derived class* or *child class* and customize it to suit your own needs. In this section, you will learn how you can inherit from the .NET Stack class, and in the next section you'll learn how you can customize it.

First, let's create a new Windows application using Visual Studio 2005. Name the project MyStackApp. Add a new class item to MyStackApp by right-clicking on the project name in Solution Explorer and then selecting Add → New Item.... Select Class and name the class *MyStack.vb*.

Double-click the *MyStack.vb* file in Solution Explorer to open it for editing. In the MyStack class, use the Inherits keyword to inherit from the Stack class, as shown in the following snippet:

```
Public Class MyStack
    Inherits System.Collections.Stack
End Class
```

By using the Inherits keyword, you specify that your MyStack class is to inherit all the methods and properties of the Stack class of the .NET Class Library. You can use MyStack in place of the Stack class. To do so, double-click on the default Form1 in Solution Explorer and then double-click on the design pane to generate the Form_Load event of Form1, as shown in Example 3-3. Enter the code as shown in bold.

Example 3-3. Replacing the Stack class with the MyStack class

```
Private Sub Form1_Load( _
    ByVal sender As System.Object, _
    ByVal e As System.EventArgs) _
    Handles MyBase.Load
    Dim ms1 As New MyStack
    ms1.Push("Hello ")
    ms1.Pop( )
End Sub
```

Customizing a Method

In the last section, you saw how to create a customized class by deriving MyStack from the .NET Stack class and how to use it just like the Stack class. However, you may wish to tweak some of the methods available in the MyStack class to suit your own purposes. Like the car designer, you might not be pleased with the performance of the braking system of the previous model. Hence, you would want to redesign and fine-tune the braking system for the new model.

Suppose you want to use a Stack to add two numbers. It turns out that the Push and Pop methods of the .NET class are not optimal for this task. Consider the following code snippet:

```
s1.Push(5)
s1.Push("S")
MsgBox(s1.Pop + s1.Pop)
```

The second Push method has pushed a String instead of an Integer onto the Stack. When you try to pop the two values (5 and S) from the stack and perform a mathematical operation on them, you will get a runtime error. This vulnerability arises from the fact that the Push method of Stack accepts an Object parameter. But of course, every .NET type is an object, so Push will accept any data type. If you know ahead of time that your stack will be used for arithmetic operations, it would be useful to restrict the parameters Push will accept to numbers only.

Changing the behavior of the inherited Push method can be done by *overriding* it. You override a method in VB 2005 by defining a new version that suits your purposes and by indicating that you want to use this version instead of the inherited version with the Overrides keyword, as shown in Example 3-4.

The first thing you will do is override the Push method in the Stack class. Recall that the Push method does not check for the type of the data pushed onto the stack. Assuming that you want the MyStack class to deal only with numeric values, you need to override the implementation of the original Push method with the Overrides keyword. Now the base method Push is no longer accessible.

Example 3-4. Overriding the Push method of Stack

```
Public Class MyStack
    Inherits System.Collections.Stack

    Public Overrides Sub Push(ByVal obj As Object)
        If Not IsNumeric(obj) Then
            Throw New Exception("Non-numeric value in Stack")
```

Example 3-4. Overriding the Push method of Stack (continued)

```
        End If
        MyBase.Push(obj)
    End Sub
End Class
```

The new Push method now checks to ensure that the value pushed into the stack is a numeric value; if it is not, the method throws an exception at runtime:

```
ms1.Push(5)
ms1.Push("S") ' runtime error
```

If the value passed to the Push method is a number, the method calls the Push method of the base class, Stack. The MyBase keyword refers to the base class from which the current class is derived, and its inherited members.

Adding Alternate Versions of a Method to a Class

Your class can offer alternate version of the same method to its users. Adding alternate versions of the same method to a class is known as *overloading* and is yet another useful object-oriented technique available to VB 2005 programmers.

Let's return to our stack example. In the previous section, you overrode the implementation of the original Push method so it will accept only numeric values. One drawback of this technique, however, is that IntelliSense will not explicitly show that numeric values are accepted (see Figure 3-1.).

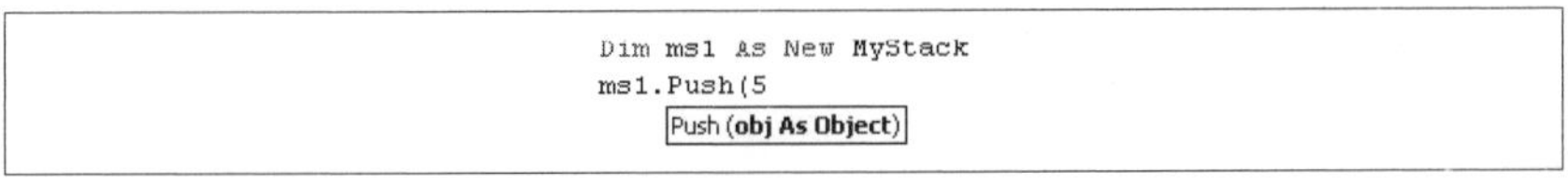

Figure 3-1. IntelliSense displaying the method signature

A better way would be to *overload* the Push method. With overloading, you can provide users with two versions of Push, each with a different signature. The *signature* of a method is determined by its parameter list. Two signatures are different when the data types or number of parameters in the parameter list are different. Example 3-5 shows how to add a new version of Push to MyStack.

Example 3-5. Overloading the Push method of MyStack

```
Public Class MyStack
    Inherits System.Collections.Stack

    Public Overrides Sub Push(ByVal obj As Object)
        If Not IsNumeric(obj) Then
```

Example 3-5. Overloading the Push method of MyStack (continued)

```
        Throw New Exception("Non-numeric value in Stack")
    End If
    MyBase.Push(obj)
End Sub

Public Overloads Sub Push(ByVal obj As Integer)
    MyBase.Push(obj)
End Sub

End Class
```

Overriding Versus Overloading

So what is the difference between Overrides and Overloads? *Overriding* means you are changing the implementation of a method, while *overloading* means adding new methods with the same name but of different signatures.

The Overloads keyword in Example 3-5 specifies that a procedure is a new version of an existing procedure with the same name. In addition to providing users with a version that accepts only integers, IntelliSense will now show that the Push method has two overloaded signatures, as shown in Figure 3-2.

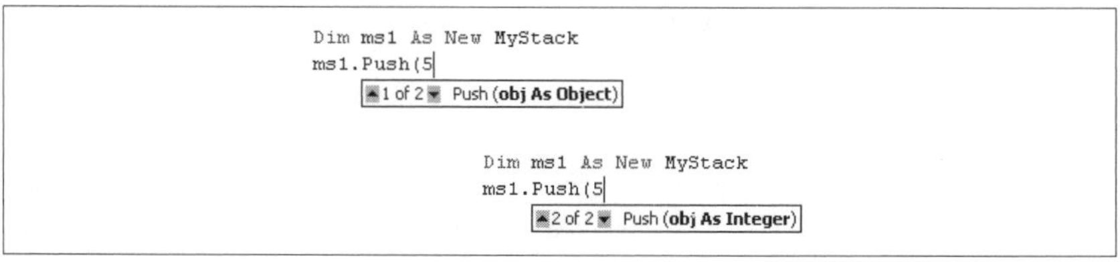

Figure 3-2. Push has two overloaded signatures

Adding a New Method

Suppose you want your new car to be available to people with special needs, such as handicapped drivers. These drivers may not be able to use the conventional brake pedals, and hence, you might need to add a special brake pedal to the steering wheel.

You can add new methods to a derived class to add functionality that's not there. For example, if you want users to push strings onto the Stack, you can define special string-friendly methods for the Push and Pop operations, as shown in Example 3-6.

VB Black Belt: Hiding a Method

Although the Overloads keyword in VB 2005 lets you define two different versions of the Push method of MyStack, because the older version is still available, it's possible to push in a non-numeric value into the Stack and cause a runtime error. A better way to prevent users from assigning a non-numeric value into the Stack would be to totally remove the original Push method that accepts the Object parameter. You can do this by using the Shadows keyword:

```
Public Class MyStack
    Inherits System.Collections.Stack

    Public Shadows Sub Push(ByVal obj As Integer)
        MyBase.Push(obj)
    End Sub

End Class
```

The Shadows keyword will hide all other methods of the same name. In this case, the Push method now has only one signature, as confirmed by IntelliSense in the figure.

```
Dim ms1 As New MyStack
ms1.Push(5
        Push (obj As Integer)
```

Example 3-6. Adding new Push and Pop methods to MyStack

```
Public Class MyStack
    Inherits System.Collections.Stack

    Public Sub PushStr(ByVal obj As String)
        MyBase.Push(obj)
    End Sub

    Public Function PopStr() As String
        Return MyBase.Pop
    End Function

End Class
```

You can use the new methods as follows:

```
Dim ms1 As New MyStack
ms1.PushStr("Hello")
MsgBox(ms1.PopStr())
```

Customizing Initialization

The purpose of a constructor is to initialize the properties of an object when it is instantiated (i.e., created).

 Constructors are optional for a class.

A constructor is a subroutine with the reserved name New. You can have as many constructors as you need so long as each has a different signature. Let's add two constructors to the MyStack class, as shown in Example 3-7.

Example 3-7. Adding a custom constructor to MyStack

```
Public Class MyStack
    Inherits System.Collections.Stack

    Public Sub New()
        '---uses the base class constructor
        MyBase.New()
    End Sub

    Public Sub New(ByVal items() As Object)
        For i As Integer = 0 To items.Length - 1
            MyBase.Push(items(i))
        Next
        ' the following will also work:
        ' MyBase.New(items)
    End Sub
    ...
```

The first constructor does not accept an input parameter, and is hence known as the *default constructor* (or *empty constructor*) of the class. The second constructor takes one parameter, items, which is then used to populate the Stack.

You can now use either of the two constructors to create an instance of the MyStack class, and the second constructor also initializes its content in a single statement, as shown in the following snippet:

```
Dim itemsArray() As Object = {"Hello", "World"}
Dim ms1 As New MyStack
Dim ms2 As New MyStack(itemsArray)
MsgBox(ms2.PopStr()) '---shows "World"
MsgBox(ms2.PopStr()) '---shows "Hello"
```

VB 6 Tip: The Sub New procedure in VB 2005 initializes objects when they are instantiated; it replaces the Class_ Initialize method used in VB 6 and earlier versions. Also, the Sub New procedure is called only when an object is instantiated; it cannot be called directly. The Class_Initialize event does not accept any arguments.

Adding Properties

The .NET Stack class exposes a number of properties, such as Count, IsSynchronized, and SyncRoot. For example, the Count property returns the number of items in the Stack. You can add additional properties to the MyStack class by using the Property keyword. For example, you might want to expose a new CountNumeric property to return the number of items in the stack that are of numeric type. You may also want to add a Description property to add a description to the class. To do so, add the code shown in bold in Example 3-8.

Example 3-8. Adding properties to MyStack

```
Public Class MyStack
    Inherits System.Collections.Stack

    Private _Description as String

    ReadOnly Property CountNumeric( ) As Integer
        Get
            Dim counter As Integer = 0
            For Each o As Object In Me
                If (IsNumeric(o)) Then
                    counter += 1
                End If
            Next
            Return counter
        End Get
    End Property

    Property Description( ) As String
        Get
            Return _Description
        End Get
        Set(ByVal value As String)
            _Description = value
        End Set
    End Property

    ...
```

ReadOnly and WriteOnly Properties

There are times when you want to allow users to read the values of a property only (and not set it). To do this, you use the ReadOnly keyword as a prefix to the property definition. Note that if you use this keyword, you cannot use a Set accessor block:

```
ReadOnly Property CountNumeric( ) As Integer
    Get
        ...
        ...
    End Get
End Property
```

Likewise, you can make a property write-only (so that people can set its value but not read it). You can do so using the WriteOnly keyword. Likewise, you cannot have the Get accessor block if you use this keyword:

```
WriteOnly Property CountNumeric( ) As Integer
    Set
        ...
        ...
    End Get
End Property
```

For a read/write property, you need both the Set and Get accessors. If you forget either one, Visual Studio 2005's new AutoCorrect feature will gladly help you to fix the missing accessor (see figure).

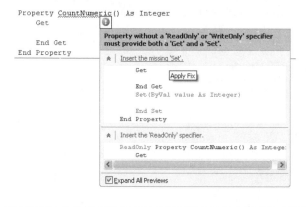

The Set and Get accessors that you define allow you to assign and retrieve values from the properties of a class. Notice that the values set for the Description property are stored internally in the private variable _Description.

The Private access modifier that precedes the declaration for _Description restricts the use of the variable to within the class. That is, they are not visible to code outside the class.

Using the Dim keyword within a class has the same effect as using the Private keyword. The following statements are equivalent:

```
Private _Description as String
    ' same as
Dim _Description as String
```

Here's a code snippet that uses the Set property procedure to assign values to the CountNumeric and Description properties and the Get property procedure to display them:

```
Dim itemsArray( ) As Object = {"Visual", "Basic", 2005}
Dim ms1 As New MyStack(itemsArray)
ms1.Description = "This is my own Stack class!"
MsgBox(ms1.CountNumeric) ' displays 1
MsgBox(ms1.Description)  ' displays "This is my own Stack class!"
```

With...End With

You can use the new VB 2005 With...End With construct to perform a series of operations on a specified object without repeatedly typing the name of the object. For example, the above could be rewritten as:

```
With ms1
    MsgBox(.CountNumeric)
    MsgBox(.Description)
End With
```

VB 6 Tip: In VB 6, you can use default properties for objects. For example, you can simply assign a string to the TextBox control, like this:

```
TextBox1="Hello World"
' equivalent to...
TextBox1.Text="Hello World"
```

This is because the Text property is the default property. The downside to using this approach is that the code is now less readable; it is much better to explicitly specify the property.

In VB 2005, default properties for controls are no longer supported.

Weakly Typed Versus Strongly Typed Variables

When you declare a variable to be of a certain data type, it is said to be *strongly typed*. For example, a variable may be declared to be of Integer type. When you declare the data type of this variable, the Visual Basic compiler performs memory allocation for the Integer data type as well as optimizations before the program is executed.

However, there are times when using a strongly typed variable isn't possible. As an example, the Push method of the Stack class accepts an item of type Object (see Figure 3-3).

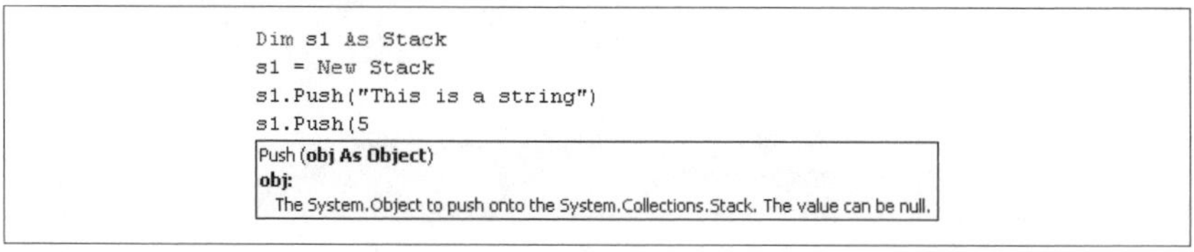

```
Dim s1 As Stack
s1 = New Stack
s1.Push("This is a string")
s1.Push(5
Push (obj As Object)
obj:
    The System.Object to push onto the System.Collections.Stack. The value can be null.
```

Figure 3-3. Pushing an Object into a Stack

You can assign the value that you have popped from the Stack into an Object variable:

```
Dim obj As Object
obj = s1.Pop
```

Because you can't determine what data type obj will be assigned to until runtime, in this case, obj is known as *weakly typed*.

The downside to using weakly typed variables is that they are less efficient (and thus slower), as doing the type conversion at runtime chews up resources. Also, a code editor feature like IntelliSense in Visual Studio will not be able to take advantage of features accorded by early binding. Figure 3-4 shows that IntelliSense does not know the properties and methods available in obj until runtime.

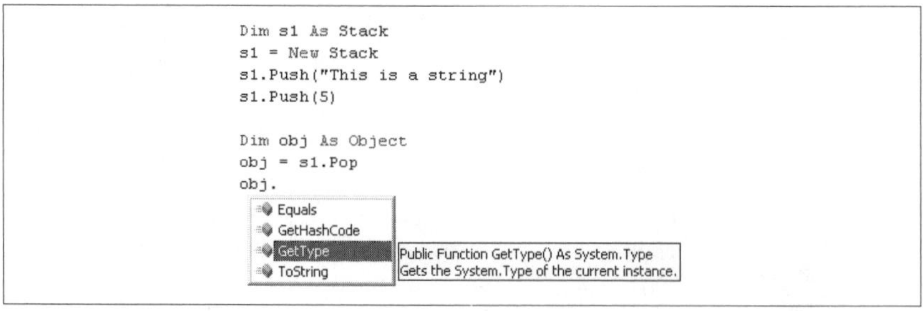

```
Dim s1 As Stack
s1 = New Stack
s1.Push("This is a string")
s1.Push(5)

Dim obj As Object
obj = s1.Pop
obj.
    Equals
    GetHashCode
    GetType          Public Function GetType() As System.Type
    ToString         Gets the System.Type of the current instance.
```

Figure 3-4. IntelliSense has no clue what data type obj is assigned to

---

However, you can perform an explicit type conversion for IntelliSense to display the properties and methods available in obj using the CType function (see Figure 3-5).

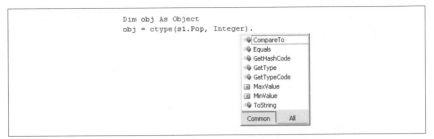

```
Dim obj As Object
obj = ctype(s1.Pop, Integer).
```

Figure 3-5. Performing an explicit type conversion using the CType function

In contrast, in the MyStack class, you have added the PushStr method, which takes in a string data type, and the PopStr method, which returns a string data type. As the type of the variable is known before the program is run, the str variable is said to be *strongly typed*:

```
Dim ms1 As New MyStack
ms1.PushStr("This is a string")

Dim str As String
str = ms1.PopStr
```

While using strongly typed variables has its disadvantages over weakly typed variables, using a weakly typed variable is useful in cases where you are writing generic code (such as the Stack class) and won't know the type of object you are working with until runtime.

Using a Generic Class

With a class like Stack, which has many uses, it would be great if you could specify the data types to be handled by a particular instance at the time the Stack object is created.

VB 2005 now supports a new feature known as *generics* and provides a number of so-called generic classes that anticipate, by design, that they will be customized before they are instantiated. Using generics, you can define classes that let you specify the data types a class accepts when the class is instantiated.

To see the benefits of generics, let's revisit the Stack class that we have been discussing in the last few sections. Without generics, you are likely to find that you need to write multiple versions of the Stack class if you want the class to work with more than one data type—say, integers, strings, or a complex Employee object. Using generics, you can now defer specifying the type of data that you want to use for your Stack until you actually instantiate a Stack object in your program. You'll find a new generic Stack class in the System.Collections.Generic namespace of the .NET Framework Class Library that allows you to specify during design time the data type you want to use. Here's how to declare that you want to push and pop integers on a stack:

```
Dim s2 As New _
    System.Collections.Generic.Stack(Of Integer)
s2.Push(5)
s2.Push(6)
s2.Push("Some string...") ' error
```

The System.Collections.Generic namespace contains generic versions of other data structures as well, such as List, Queue, Dictionary, and more.

By using the new Of keyword, you indicate the type of data you want to use with that class.

If you turn Option Strict On, the code editor will underline the third Push method call, indicating that it is an error to push in a string data type.

If you want to use the Stack class for String data types, you simply do this:

```
Dim s2 As New _
    System.Collections.Generic.Stack(Of String)
s2.Push("VB2005 ")
s2.Push("supports ")
s2.Push("Generics")
```

Besides using the generic classes in the .NET Framework, you can also write your own generic classes, a topic that is beyond the scope of this book. (For additional information, see *Programming Visual Basic 2005*, O'Reilly.)

Splitting Up the Physical Implementation of a Class

VB 2005 supports a new .NET 2.0 enhancement: *partial classes*. In a nutshell, with partial classes, you can now split your class definition into multiple physical files. Logically, partial classes do not make any difference to the compiler. During compile time, the Visual Basic compiler simply groups all the various partial classes together and treats them as a single entity.

One of the greatest benefits of partial classes is that they allow a clean separation of business logic and the user interface (in particular, the code that is generated by the visual designer in Visual Studio 2005).

Using partial classes, the UI code can be hidden from the developer, who usually has no need to access it anyway. Partial classes also make debugging easier, as the code is partitioned into separate files.

Figure 3-6 shows the code behind of a Windows Form: Form1. Notice that no hidden Windows designer-generated code appears on the page (as would be visible in Visual Studio .NET 2003). The absence of that section allows you to concentrate on writing the business logic of your application and reduces the chances that you may inadvertently modify the code generated by the designer.

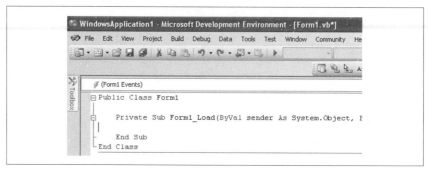

Figure 3-6. The code behind of Form1

If for some reason you need to access the Windows designer-generated code, you can go to Solution Explorer and click on the Show All Files button. There you will find a file named *Form1.Designer.vb* (see Figure 3-7) under the *Form1.vb* file.

Figure 3-7. Revealing the Windows designer-generated code in Solution Explorer

Figure 3-8 shows the content of the *Form1.Designer.vb* file.

In VB 2005, all of the partial classes except one must use the Partial keyword prefix; only one class may omit it. However, it is recommended that you always prefix all your partial classes with the Partial keyword. At least this will give you a visual clue that part of the implementation of the class lies somewhere else, and this is definitely useful when it comes to debugging.

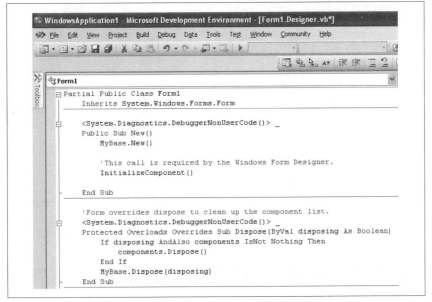

Figure 3-8. The content of the Windows designer-generated code

 While partial classes allow you to split the definition of a class into multiple files, you cannot mix languages. That is, all partial classes must be written in the same language. Besides using the Partial keyword for classes, you can also use it for structures and interfaces.

If your class implements many interfaces (see "Creating Contracts with Implementers Using Interfaces" for more details on interfaces), it is a good idea to use a partial class to contain the implementation for each interface.

Designing Your Own Classes

While the My objects and the hundreds of types in the .NET Framework Class Library provide ready-to-use solutions to many of the tasks you need to perform in a Visual Basic application, at some point you'll need to create your own classes. In this section, you'll see how to do that. You'll also see how you can control access to the variables and methods in your classes, and when it might make sense to use a Structure—a "light-weight" class—instead.

Defining a Class

Before you build a car, you need a design. The design of a car specifies its properties, its behaviors, and how it works internally. Likewise, to design a class of your own, you need to specify the methods and properties, as well as the internal workings of the class.

To see how to define a class, let's create a Stack class of our own. In the following steps, you'll use the Visual Studio 2005 class designer to get the work done.

1. Using Visual Studio 2005, create a new Windows application. Name the project StackClassApp.

2. Add a new class file to the project by right-clicking on the project name in Solution Explorer and then selecting Add → New Item.... Select the Class template and name it *StackClass.vb*. Click Add (see Figure 3-9).

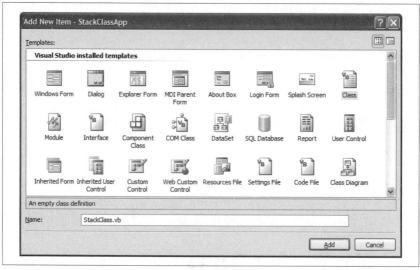

Figure 3-9. Adding a new class file to the project

3. The *StackClass.vb* file will now be opened in Visual Studio 2005, ready to be edited. You can either define your class by coding directly into the open *StackClass.vb* file, or use the Class Designer to do the job. Let's first take a look at the Class Designer.

 The Class Designer is not included in the Visual Basic 2005 Express Edition. If you are using Visual Basic 2005 Express Edition, please skip to Step 6.

4. To use the Class Designer, right-click on *StackClass.vb* in Solution Explorer and then select View Class Diagram, as shown in Figure 3-10.

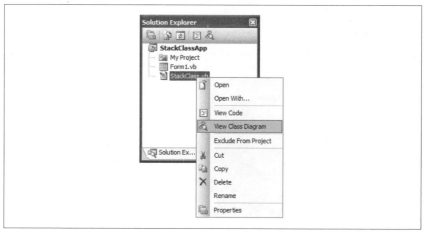

Figure 3-10. Invoking the Class Designer

5. The Class Designer will display a rectangular box showing the empty StackClass class. To add methods, properties, and more to the class, right-click on the class rectangle and select Add, as shown in Figure 3-11, and select the elements you wish to add.

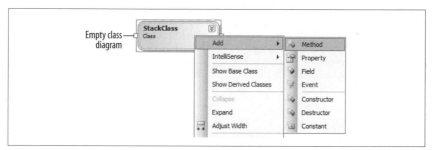

Figure 3-11. Modifying the class

Figure 3-12 shows what the completed class diagram for StackClass might look like after you've added the methods, properties, and other elements called for in your design. You can use the Properties window to customize each element (such as access mode, data type, etc.). However, when defining a relatively simple class, like the StackClass, it is faster to type the code in directly, as you'll do in the next step. The Class Designer is useful when you have several classes and you want to view their relationship visually.

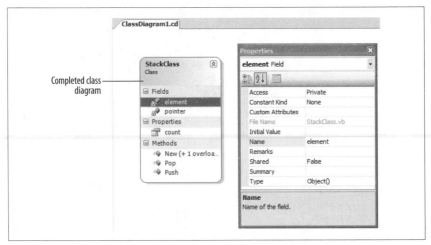

Figure 3-12. Adding the various methods, properties, and fields to the StackClass class

6. Let's abandon the Class Designer, open *StackClass.vb*, and simply type
   the code shown in Example 3-9 into the file.

Example 3-9. The definition for the StackClass class

```
Public Class StackClass
    '---stores the items in the stack
    Private element() As Object
    '---indicate the current stack pointer
    Private pointer As Integer

    '---instantiates and specify the default size of the stack
    Public Sub New()
        ReDim element(100)
        pointer = 0
    End Sub

    '---instantiates and specify the size of the stack
    Public Sub New(ByVal size As Integer)
        ReDim element(size - 1)
        pointer = 0
    End Sub

    '---push an item into the stack
    Public Sub Push(ByVal item As Object)
        If pointer > UBound(element) Then
            Throw New Exception("Stack is full.")
        End If
        element(pointer) = item
        pointer += 1
    End Sub
```

Example 3-9. The definition for the StackClass class (continued)

```
    '---pop an item from the stack
    Public Function Pop( ) As Object
        pointer -= 1
        If pointer < 0 Then
            Throw New Exception("Stack is empty.")
        End If
        Return element(pointer)
    End Function

    '---return the number of items in the stack
    ReadOnly Property count( ) As Integer
        Get
            Return pointer
        End Get
    End Property
End Class
```

Observe that StackClass contains the following elements:

- Two private variables (element and pointer) that are used internally to store the items in a stack. The Private keyword indicates that the variables are visible only within the class and cannot be accessed outside the class.

- Two constructors (New) that initialize the object when it is instantiated.

- Two methods (a subroutine and a function) for pushing (Push) and popping (Pop) items in and out of the stack. The Public keyword indicates that the methods are accessible outside the class.

- One read-only property that returns the number of items in the stack.

Controlling Access to Class Members

Variables, classes, and members can be declared to be public or private using the Public and Private access modifiers. Access modifiers restrict the scope of member variables in a class. For example, a variable defined with the Private keyword is visible only within the class in which it is defined. A Public variable, on the other hand, is visible outside the class. Declaring a private variable is useful in cases where you do not want users who are using your class to know about the detailed workings of your class.

There are two more access modifiers that you can use:

- Protected

- Friend

To see how these two access modifiers affect the scope of variables, classes, and member variables, consider the following example.

Suppose you have the following class definition:

```
Public Class BMW
    Friend var1 As Integer
    Protected var2 As Integer
    Private var3 As Integer
    Public var4 As Integer
End Class
```

Within the class, you have four variables each declared with a different access modifier. Create an instance of class BMW and try to assign values to the member variables:

```
Dim objA As New BMW
objA.var1 = 1
objA.var2 = 2 ' Error; not allowed
objA.var3 = 3 ' Error; not allowed
objA.var4 = 4
```

You will notice that var2 and var3 are not accessible because:

- var2 is declared with the Protected access modifier. The Protected access modifier works like the Private access modifier, which means that the variable is not visible outside the class. However, the difference between Protected and Private is that variables declared Protected are visible within their own class or subclasses. You will see more of this in the next example.

- var3 is a private variable.

Consider the following example, where class MiniCooper inherits from class BMW:

```
Public Class MiniCooper
    Inherits BMW
    Public Sub doSomething()
        MyBase.var1 = 1
        MyBase.var2 = 2
        MyBase.var3 = 3   'Error; not allowed
        MyBase.var4 = 4
    End Sub
End Class
```

Within class MiniCooper, you have a method doSomething that tries to access the four variables in the base class. Notice that var2 is accessible but var3 is not. This is because:

- var2 is visible within the subclasses of class BMW. Hence, var2 is accessible.

- var3 is a private variable.

In the two examples above, you may notice that var1 is visible all along. Basically, the Friend and the Public access modifiers are similar with the exception that Friend variables are accessible from within their declaration context and from anywhere else in the same program (but not outside the program).

You can combine the two access modifiers, Protected and Friend, together to give a variable both protected and friend access. For example, here var2 is now declared as Protected Friend:

```
Public Class BMW
    Friend var1 As Integer
    Protected Friend var2 As Integer
    Private var3 As Integer
    Public var4 As Integer
End Class
```

This means that var2 is visible within the subclass and also visible within the same program. The following code example shows that now var2 is visible within the same program:

```
Dim objA As New BMW
objA.var1 = 1
objA.var2 = 2 ' Allowed!
objA.var3 = 3 ' Error; not allowed
objA.var4 = 4
```

Aggregating Data Types Using a Structure

Sometimes you need to represent a piece of information using multiple data types, but don't necessarily want the overhead of defining a class and managing an object. For example, suppose you need to maintain information about the different types of car owned by a company, such as model and year of registration. In this case, you can either use a class or a *structure* to aggregate all the required information.

In VB 2005, a structure is implemented using the Structure keyword. In VB 6, you define structure using the Type...End Type syntax, which is no longer supported in VB 2005.

Example 3-10 shows the definition for a Structure named Car.

Example 3-10. Declaring a structure

```
Structure Car
    Public Model As String
    Public Year As UShort
End Structure
```

Note that in a Structure, you can define properties and methods just like in a class.

To use a Structure, you simply declare variables to be of the structure type, as shown in Example 3-11.

Example 3-11. Using structures

```
Dim Car1, Car2 As Car

Car1.Model = "Nissan Maxima"
Car1.Year = 2004

Car2 = Car1
Car2.Model = "Toyota Camry"
```

Example 3-11 creates two variables of type Car. The first variable is initialized and then copied to the second variable. Because structure is a value type, changes to the second variable do not affect the first member (see Figure 3-13).

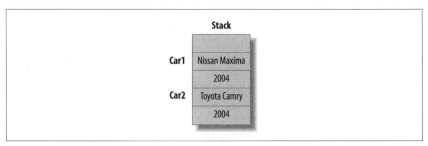

Figure 3-13. Memory storage for a structure

So, what is the difference between a class and a structure? A class is a reference type, which means that the actual storage of an object is on the heap with the object variable on the stack pointing to it. A structure, on the other hand, is a value type, and its value is stored directly on the stack.

You should use a structure when:

- You have a small amount of data.
- You perform a large number of operations on each instance; in this case, performance is much faster than using a class.
- You have no need to inherit the structure.

A class is preferred when:

- You need to use inheritance for complex data types.
- You need to initialize one or more members at creation time.

Controlling How Classes Are Implemented

Although you can generally create custom versions of any of classes that you write or find in the .NET Class Libraries, there will be times when you'll want to control the outcome, especially when others will use your work. There are also times when you'll want to prove to .NET that your class has fulfilled the terms of a contract that promises a certain level of functionality and is therefore qualified to handle particular assignments.

Allowing or Preventing Overridable Methods

In the earlier part of this chapter, you saw how to use the Stack class in the System.Collections namespace and how you can extend its functionality by inheriting from it. You were also able to override and overload some of its methods to suit your own requirements.

In this section, you will learn how you can create classes from which others can inherit. You will also learn how to specially allow or prevent subclasses from changing your methods.

Using the StackClass defined in the last section, suppose you want others, including yourself, to be able to reuse the class and override its methods. In this case, you would do the following:

```
Public Class MyStackClass
    Inherits StackClass

End Class
```

To override the Push and Pop methods in the base class, you would use the Overrides keyword, as shown in Example 3-12.

Example 3-12. Overriding the Push and Pop methods of MyStackClass

```
Public Class MyStackClass
    Inherits StackClass
    Public Overrides Sub Push(ByVal item As Object)
        ...
        MyBase.Push(item)
    End Sub

    Public Overrides Function Pop( ) As Object
        ...
        Return MyBase.Pop( )
    End Function
End Class
```

However, for the Push and Pop methods to be overridden in the base class, you need to give clients permission to do so by adding the Overridable keyword, as shown in Example 3-13.

 Without the Overridable keyword, you would not be able to override the methods in the base class.

Example 3-13. Making the Push and Pop methods of StackClass overridable

```
Public Class StackClass
    ...
    Public Overridable Sub Push(ByVal item As Object)
        If pointer > UBound(element) Then
            Throw New Exception("Stack is full.")
        End If
        element(pointer) = item
        pointer += 1
    End Sub

    Public Overridable Function Pop( ) As Object
        pointer -= 1
        If pointer < 0 Then
            Throw New Exception("Stack is empty.")
        End If
        Return element(pointer)
    End Function
End Class
```

In this case, the implementations of the methods are provided, and classes that inherit from them can choose to override this implementation if they want to.

Specifying Implementation Details with Abstract Classes and Methods

Suppose one day your designer receives a call from a customer who wants the designer to create a custom car for him. He may tell the designer what his requirements are and what features that he wants for that car, but he does not tell the designer what to do, since it is the designer's job to figure out implementation. In this case, what the customer provides is essentially an *abstract class* (the request to design a car) along with a list of various *abstract methods* (the features of the car).

There are times when you will want to define the structure of a class and leave it to a subclass to provide its implementation. For example, you might want to define the methods available in a Stack class but leave the implementation to the subclass (so that implementers can use whatever data structures they prefer to implement the Stack, such as an array). Here's an example of how to do it:

```
Public MustInherit Class AbstractStackClass
    Public MustOverride Sub Push(ByVal item As Object)
    Public MustOverride Function Pop() As Object
End Class
```

The MustInherit keyword specifies that the AbstractStackClass class cannot be directly instantiated. The class can be used only if inherited by a subclass. Thus, the following is not valid:

```
Dim s1 As New AbstractStackClass '<--not allowed
```

The purpose of this class is to provide the base properties and methods for subclasses.

The Push and Pop methods are known as *abstract methods*. You do not implement an abstract method when you declare it; its implementation is left to the classes that inherit from it. It is logical for this method to be abstract, because the way you push or pop an item into a Stack is dependent on how you implement a Stack internally. You declare an abstract method in VB 2005 with the MustOverride keyword.

To implement the class and its methods, you then inherit from the AbstractStackClass, and then provide the implementation of the methods using the Overrides keyword, as shown in Example 3-14. You can also add additional methods and constructors to the class.

Example 3-14. Implementing the AbstractStackClass abstract class

```
Public Class MyStackClass
    Inherits AbstractStackClass

    Private element() As Object
    Private pointer As Integer
    Public Sub New()
        ReDim element(100)
        pointer = 0
    End Sub

    Public Sub New(ByVal size As Integer)
        ReDim element(size - 1)
        pointer = 0
    End Sub

    Public Overrides Sub Push(ByVal item As Object)
        If pointer > UBound(element) Then
            Throw New Exception("Stack is full.")
        End If
```

Example 3-14. Implementing the AbstractStackClass abstract class (continued)

```
            element(pointer) = item
            pointer += 1
    End Sub

    Public Overrides Function Pop( ) As Object
            pointer -= 1
            If pointer < 0 Then
                Throw New Exception("Stack is empty.")
            End If
            Return element(pointer)
    End Function

End Class
```

Note that in an abstract class, you can still provide implementations for some methods so that subclasses can use them; not all methods must be abstract.

Creating Contracts with Implementers Using Interfaces

An interface is similar to the abstract class, with one notable difference: an interface contains no implementation at all, while an abstract class may specify one or more method implementations.

Consider the interface example in Example 3-15.

Example 3-15. Defining an interface for StackClass

```
Interface IStack
    Sub Push(ByVal item As Object)
    Function Pop( ) As Object
End Interface
```

To implement the interface and the methods contained within it, use the Implements keyword, as shown in Example 3-16.

Abstract Classes Versus Interfaces

The advantage of using an interface is that a class can implement multiple interfaces, but can never inherit from more than a single class at the same time. However, when you implement an interface (or interfaces), you need to implement all of the methods specified by the interface, since the interface itself cannot have any implementation. An abstract class, on the other hand, can define the implementation for some of its methods, but you can only inherit from one abstract class.

Example 3-16. Implementing the IStack interface

```
Public Class MyStackClass
    Implements IStack

    Public Function Pop( ) As Object Implements IStack.Pop
        ...
    End Function

    Public Sub Push(ByVal item As Object) Implements IStack.Push
        ...
    End Sub
End Class
```

 VB 2005 allows you to implement multiple interfaces.

Controlling the Destruction of Objects

To *dereference* an object—i.e., remove the reference to an object that you have created—you can simply set the object variable to Nothing, like this:

```
Dim ms1 As New MyStack( )
ms1 = Nothing
```

 To dereference an object, you need not necessarily set it to Nothing. When an object variable goes out of scope (such as when reaching the end of a function), the variable will be dereferenced automatically.

Once an object is dereferenced, the runtime will perform a garbage collection when the memory pressure gets high enough (i.e., the system begins to run out of memory) to reclaim the memory used by the object. The garbage collector will call the Finalize method. You cannot call it directly.

 It is not guaranteed that the Finalize method will be called immediately when an object is dereferenced. This timing of this is entirely up to the garbage collector in the CLR.

The Finalize method is a good place for you to place code that frees up resources, especially if your object uses *unmanaged objects* (such as database handles or COM objects, and so on; the resources used by these objects would not be freed up automatically):

```
Protected Overrides Sub Finalize( )
    ' code to release objects explicitly

End Sub
```

VB 6 Tip: The Sub Finalize procedure in VB 2005 replaces the Class_Terminate method used in VB 6 and earlier versions. However, unlike the Class_Terminate method, the Finalize procedure is not guaranteed to execute immediately after setting an object to Nothing.

Because calling the Finalize method will add overhead to the execution of your application, you should implement Finalize only when necessary. Also, the Finalize method is not guaranteed to ever be called; it depends on the shutdown conditions of the runtime.

Since you can't really determine when an object's resource will be freed up, you can use the second type of method supported in VB 2005, the Dispose method, and place your code for freeing up the resources there. To use the Dispose method, you need to implement the IDisposable interface and implement the IDisposable.Dispose method, as shown in Example 3-17.

Example 3-17. Using the Dispose method

```
Public Class MyStack
    Inherits Stack
    Implements IDisposable
    ...
    Protected Overrides Sub Finalize( )
        ' code to release objects explicitly

    End Sub

    Public Sub Dispose( ) Implements _
        IDisposable.Dispose
        ' code to release objects explicitly

    End Sub
    ...
```

The advantage of using the Dispose method is that you can explicitly call it to free up all your resources:

```
ms1.Dispose( )
```

When you do not call the Dispose method explicitly, you should also call it in Finalize. (Note that in Example 3-17, you make a call to the Dispose method in the Finalize method.) Hence, you need to make sure that the code in the Dispose method is safe to be called multiple times.

Disposing of Resources

Often you need to create and use some resources and then immediately release the resources so that memory can be reclaimed. VB 2005 comes with a new construct known as Using...End Using. The Using...End Using construct guarantees that the resources acquired within the Using block will be disposed of after the execution of the block. Consider the following:

```
Public Sub Data_Access( _
    ByVal str As String)
    Using conn As New SqlConnection(str)
        Dim ds As DataSet
        '---some code to perform data
        ' access
    End Using
    ...
    ...
End Sub
```

The conn and ds objects are valid only within the Using block. The conn object will be disposed after the execution of the Using block (its Dispose method will get called). The Using block is a good way for you to ensure that resources (especially COM objects and unmanaged code, which would not be unloaded automatically by the garbage collector in the CLR) are properly disposed of after they are no longer needed.

Tagging Objects with Attributes

Attributes are descriptive tags that can be used in VB 2005 applications to provide additional information about types (classes), fields, methods, and properties. Attributes can be used by .NET to decide how to handle objects while an application is running.

Using our car example, the cars of ambassadors often display a flag indicating their status as VIPs so that motorists will give way when they approach. The flag in this case can be likened to an attribute.

Using attributes—either those provided by the .NET Framework or those you define yourself—gives you additional control over the objects in your applications. Attributes in Visual Basic are used in web services. For example, suppose you wish to expose a Translate method in an ASP.NET Web Service project. Prefixing the method with the <WebMethod( )> attribute will expose the method as a web service using SOAP, as shown in Example 3-18.

Example 3-18. Using the WebMethod attribute

```
<WebMethod( )> _
Public Function Translate(ByVal str As String) _
    As String
    ...
End Function
```

Another occasion on which you're likely to use attributes is when you need to use a legacy unmanaged DLL to perform some function in a .NET application. To import the relevant function, you'll need to use the <DllImport( )> attribute, as shown in Example 3-19.

Example 3-19. Using the DllImport attribute

```
<DllImport("KERNEL32.DLL", EntryPoint:="MoveFileW", _
    SetLastError:=True, CharSet:=CharSet.Unicode, _
    ExactSpelling:=True, _
    CallingConvention:=CallingConvention.StdCall)> _
Public Shared Function MoveFile(ByVal src As String, _
                                ByVal dst As String) _
                                As Boolean
    ' Leave function empty - DLLImport attribute forwards
    ' calls to MoveFile to MoveFileW in KERNEL32.DLL.
End Function
```

> To use the <DllImport( )> attribute, you need to import the System.Runtime.InteropServices namespace in your project.

In Visual Studio 2005, you can use attributes to mark a method in a class as obsolete. Marking a method with the <Obsolete( )> intrinsic attribute causes a warning message to be displayed when someone attempts to use it, as shown in Example 3-20.

Example 3-20. Using the Obsolete intrinsic attribute

```
Public Class MyStack
    ...
    <Obsolete("This method is obsolete. Use Push(obj as Object)")> _
    Public Sub PushStr(ByVal obj As String)
        MyBase.Push(obj)
    End Sub
    ...
```

Suppose now you tried to use the PushStr method of the MyStack class:

```
        Dim ms2 As New MyStack( )
        ms2.PushStr("Hello")
```

Visual Studio 2005 will signal a warning (not an error though) in the Error List window (see Figure 3-14).

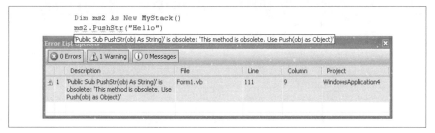

Figure 3-14. The Error List window displaying the warning on the obsolete method

A more thorough discussion of attributes is beyond the scope of this book. For additional information, see *Programming Visual Basic 2005* by Jesse Liberty (O'Reilly) or *Programming .NET Components* by Juval Lowy (O'Reilly).

Summary

This chapter has explored several concepts central to the practice of OOP and demonstrated how you can use them with VB 2005. Here is what you have learned:

- The benefits of using the OOP features of VB 2005, especially code reuse

- How to create a new class using the Class Designer and the VB 2005 language, and how to instantiate it at runtime

- How to extend an existing class by inheriting from it and overriding or overloading its methods

- Enhancements to VB 2005 that provide additional support for code reuse: generics and partial classes

- Advanced OO techniques for controlling how classes are implemented and objects are handled at runtime, such as the use of abstract classes and methods, interfaces, attributes, and access modifiers

In the next chapter, you will learn more about what's new in Windows development in VB 2005 and see how to put the VB 2005 language and its new support for OOP to work.

CHAPTER 4

Developing a Windows Application

Now that you've become familiar with the latest features of the VB 2005 language and the new productivity tools added to Visual Studio 2005, it's time to build a complete application.

In this chapter, you will build a Windows application that you can use to create an online catalog of the books you own. The catalog stores details such as the ISBN (the book industry standard number used to uniquely identify a book), title, authors, publisher, and price of each volume in your collection. The application lets you search Amazon.com for information about particular titles by entering keywords in a search window. You can then store that information, including images of the book covers, in a personal database on your Windows workstation or PC.

Later in the chapter, you'll add a second window to the application that lets users display the complete catalog of books stored in the local database and to display the details of any particular title.

Figure 4-1 shows the main window of the finished application. The window includes two panels: a panel on the left for showing the results of Amazon.com keyword searches that you enter and a panel on the right for displaying the details of a particular book returned by the search. The main window contains the usual features you expect to find in a Windows application such as a menu, a toolbar, and a status bar. Figure 4-30 shows the finished application with both windows open.

You will build the application using several of the latest Visual Studio 2005 controls, including the SplitContainer, MenuStrip, ToolStrip, and StatusStrip controls. You will also work with data access controls and wizards that simplify the use of the ADO.NET classes for data access. You will use the Amazon.com web service to retrieve detailed information about your books and then save it for offline viewing, and you'll see how easy it is to incorporate a web service in an application with Visual Studio 2005. Though multithreading has traditionally been seen as a black art, the new BackgroundWorker control reduces its use to a drag-and-drop operation. You'll use multithreading to keep the UI of your Windows application responsive while it's accessing the Amazon.com web service.

Once the library application is complete, you will use ClickOnce, a new smart client deployment technique in the .NET Framework 2.0, to post it to an IIS host. ClickOnce is not only an easier way to deploy Windows applications that make use of the Internet, but ClickOnce also ensures that the user will be notified whenever an updated version of the application is posted to the server. You'll use this feature to deploy an updated version of the library application at the end of this chapter.

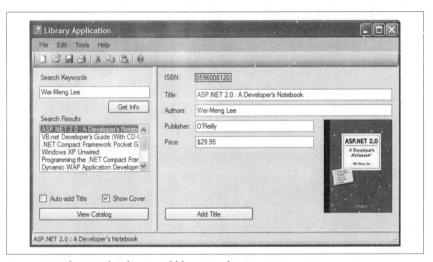

Figure 4-1. The completed personal library application

Creating the Windows Application and Building the Main Window

The first step toward building the library application is to use Visual Studio 2005 to create a new Windows application project and then build the main window. You'll use a variety of new controls that ship with Visual Basic 2005 to get the job done.

1. Launch Visual Studio 2005 and create a new Windows application by selecting File → New Project. Choose the Visual Basic/Windows project type in the Project types dialog panel and select the Windows Application template in the Templates panel, as shown in Figure 4-2. Name the

project *LibraryApp*. Click OK. Visual Studio will create the project and display a blank form with the default name Form1.vb [Design]. Project files are displayed in the Solution Explorer window to the right of the form design page. You can access the properties of Form1 in the Properties window, also to the right of the form design page. To give the application a public name, set the name of Form1 to "Library Application" by entering the string as its Text property in the Properties window. When the main application window displays, this name will appear in its titlebar.

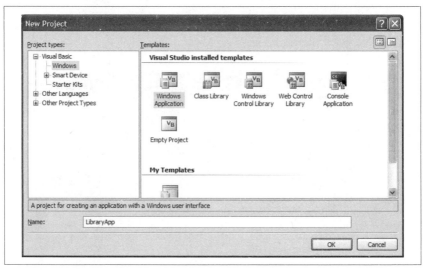

Figure 4-2. Creating a new Windows application project

2. Now you're ready to construct the application main window. You'll begin by adding an Office style menu to Form1. Click on the Toolbox tab to the left of the Form1 designer page and drag-and-drop a MenuStrip control from the Menus & Toolbars tab onto Form1. The empty menu bar is automatically placed at the top of the page, and an icon for the control appears in a strip at the bottom of the designer page. You can display the Properties window for the control by clicking either the empty bar or the control icon.

Click on the Insert Standard Items link in the MenuStrip Tasks menu to insert the commonly used File, Edit, Tools, and Help menus, as shown in Figure 4-3.

3. Next, add a toolbar to the window by dragging-and-dropping the ToolStrip control from the Menus & Toolbars tab in the Toolbox onto Form1. Click on the Insert Standard Items link to add the list of commonly used toolbar icons as shown in Figure 4-4.

Figure 4-3. Adding a MenuStrip control to the form

Figure 4-4. Adding a ToolStrip control to the form

The new MenuStrip and ToolStrip controls in VB 2005 make it much easier for developers to create professional looking Windows applications.

4. The design for the main window shown in Figure 4-1 calls for a status bar that we'll use to show progress in gathering information from Amazon.com when a user initiates a search. You'll build the bar by dragging-and-dropping a StatusStrip control onto Form1, and then add a StatusLabel control by selecting the StatusLabel item from the StatusStrip drop-down listbox, as shown in Figure 4-5. The StatusLabel control works like any Label control.

Figure 4-5. Inserting StatusLabel and ProgressBar controls into the StatusStrip control

5. To create the separate search and book details panels shown in Figure 4-1, drag-and-drop a SplitContainer control from the Containers tab of the Toolbox onto Form1. The SplitContainer control represents a control consisting of a movable bar that divides a container's display area into two resizable panels. Set the BorderStyle property of the SplitContainer control to "Fixed3D" so that it shows a three-dimensional border.

 The SplitContainer control is new in VB 2005 and is a much improved version of its predecessor.

At this point, your application window should look like the one shown in Figure 4-6.

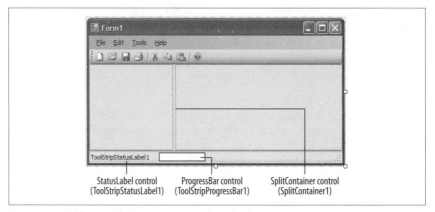

Figure 4-6. Adding a SplitContainer control to the form

6. Populate the left panel of the SplitContainer control with the controls as shown in Figure 4-7 by dragging-and-dropping each control from the Toolbox onto the form. Name the controls as shown by clicking on each control and setting its Name property in the Properties window.

Creating a Database to Store Books Information

The information about each book that a user acquires from Amazon.com needs to be saved to a local database on the PC or workstation. To provide this functionality, you need to add a database to your project. For this project, you'll use a SQL database file to store your book data. Once you've created the database file, you'll add a table to store the individual records for each book in your collection.

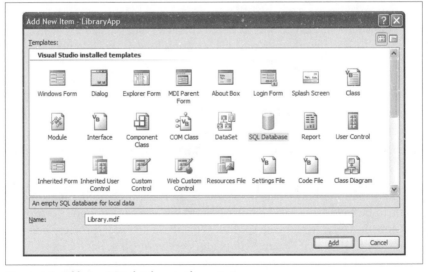

Figure 4-7. *Populating the left panel of the SplitContainer control*

1. To add a database file to your project, first right-click on the project name, LibraryApp, in Solution Explorer and then select Add → New Item.... Now, in the Add New Item dialog box, select SQL Database and set the Name of the database file to *Library.mdf*, as shown in Figure 4-8. Click Add.

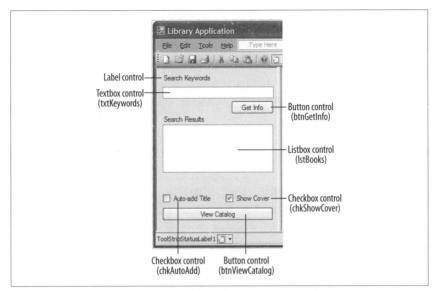

Figure 4-8. *Adding a SQL database to the project*

The *Library.mdf* database file icon will now appear in the Solution Explorer window, and the Data Source Configuration Wizard will appear. As you won't be using this wizard, click Cancel.

2. Now you're ready to create the table to hold the records for the books in your library. Double-click the *Library.mdf* file icon to view it in more detail in the Database Explorer as shown in Figure 4-9.

   Expand the *Library.mdf* file, right-click on the Tables subfolder icon, and select Add New Table. Visual Studio 2005 creates the table and displays a blank page (*dbo: Table 1*) that you'll use to define its records.

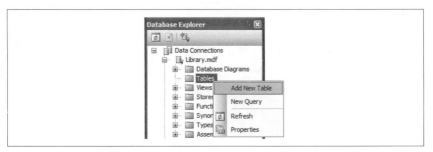

Figure 4-9. Adding a new table to the database

With a blank table in hand, you'll now define its columns and fields. Enter the name of each field as shown in Figure 4-10. After entering a name, tab to the right to enter a data type. You can type in the data type shown in Figure 4-10, or select it from the drop-down menu provided by Visual Studio 2005. You'll need to enter the Data Type for Title and Publisher manually to specify a 100 character length. Tab to the last column to specify whether null values are allowed. By default, they are. The ISBN field contains the primary key for each record. Select and right-click on the field and select Set Primary Key from the drop-down menu. Uncheck the Allow Nulls box for the field since it would be unacceptable to have a record in the database without a primary key. Figure 4-10 shows the completed page.

Save the table by selecting "Save Table 1" from the File menu. When prompted, name the table *Titles*.

Close the table window by right-clicking on its title tab and selecting Close.

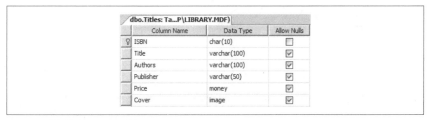

Figure 4-10. Defining a table

Binding Library Data to the Form

You will now use the data-binding features of VB 2005 to bind the database that you have just created to the form. To do so, you need to add a data source to the Data Sources window.

1. Go to Data → Show Data Sources to display the Data Sources window.

2. Click on the Add New Data Source button at the top of the Data Sources window to add a new data source, as shown in Figure 4-11.

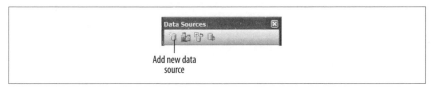

Figure 4-11. Adding a new data source

The Data Source Configuration Wizard will appear. Select Database as the Data Source type and click Next.

3. When the "Choose your data connection" dialog appears, you will notice that the *Library.mdf* file has already been selected, as shown in Figure 4-12). Click Next.

4. Now you have the option to save the connection string that the page will use to connect to the *Library.mdf* database in the application configuration file. This option allows you to change the database details easily without recompiling the application even after it has been deployed. This is the default, so leave the checkbox checked and click Next to go to the next step.

5. In the next window, the "Choose your database objects dialog," you can select the table(s) you want to work with. For this project, check the *Titles* table, which contains the records for your stored books. This step is as shown in Figure 4-13.

Figure 4-12. Selecting the data connection

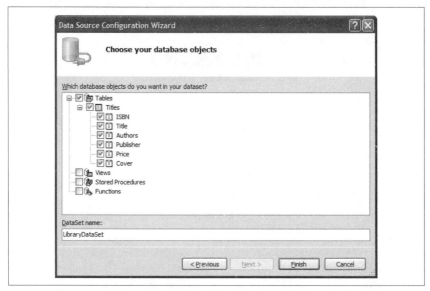

Figure 4-13. Selecting the table to work with

That's it! You've configured the *Library.mdf* database file as a data source without writing a line of code. Now click Finish.

You should now see the *Titles* table displayed as a tree in the Data Sources window, as shown in Figure 4-14.

Remember to close the table window as described in step 2 of the section "Creating a Database to Store Books Information." Otherwise, the Data Sources window will not display the icons next to the table and fields.

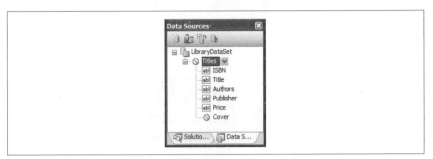

Figure 4-14. The Titles table in the Data Sources window

6. You will now change the binding of some of the fields in the table in the Data Sources window. Change the binding of the *ISBN* field from TextBox to Label so that the ISBN of a book is displayed in a non-editable Label control (see Figure 4-15). Also, change the binding of the *Cover* field from None to PictureBox. Doing so will display the data contained in the *Cover* field in a PictureBox control.

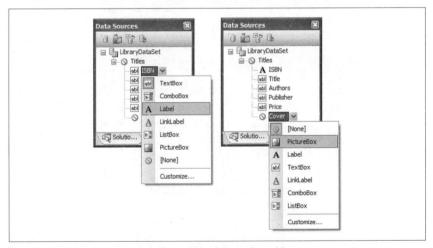

Figure 4-15. Changing the default binding of the Titles table

7. Drag-and-drop the *ISBN, Title, Authors, Publisher, Price,* and *Cover* fields (individually) from the *Titles* table in the Data Sources window onto the right panel of the SplitContainer control. Also, add in a Button control named Add Title. The form should now look like the one shown in Figure 4-16. Name the controls as shown in the figure callouts (the names appear in parentheses).

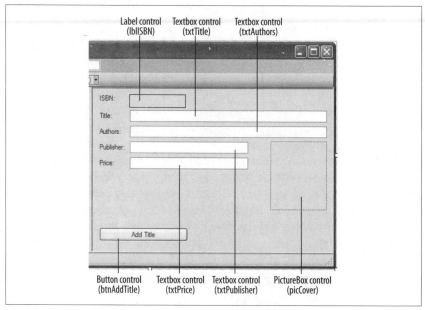

Figure 4-16. Populating the form with the various controls

8. You will notice that a couple of controls appeared at the bottom of the *Form1.vb* design page (see Figure 4-17). These controls perform all the magic of binding the data in your database to the controls on your form. Going into the details of what they do specifically is beyond the scope of this book.

Figure 4-17. The controls added at the bottom of Form1.vb

9. You will also notice that a control known as the BindingNavigator control is added to the form when you drag-and-drop the fields from the Data Sources window onto the form (see Figure 4-18). This control allows users to navigate through the records in the database. As we are not going to let the user view the list of books in this window, the control is not relevant in this case. So, set its Visible property to False so that it will not display on the form. Alternatively, you can just delete it.

Figure 4-18. The BindingNavigator control added to the form

10. Once you've completed the Library Application form, you need to set a few of the properties of the newly added controls. First, you'll want to set the Anchor property of each control to ensure that each is correctly resized and positioned when a user resizes the form. The Anchor property of a control determines where it should be positioned when the form is resized. For example, if a control's Anchor property is set to Top, Left, the control's position will be fixed. However, if its Anchor property is set to Bottom, Right, its position will be anchored to the bottom-right corner of the form (see Figure 4-19).

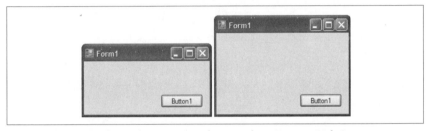

Figure 4-19. Setting the Anchor property of a control to "Bottom, Right"

If the Anchor property is set to Top, Left, Right, the control will be resized horizontally when the form is resized (see Figure 4-20).

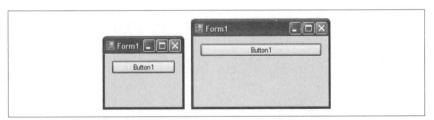

Figure 4-20. Setting the Anchor property of a control to "Top, Left, Right"

If the Anchor property is set to Top, Bottom, Left, Right, the control will be resized both vertically and horizontally when the form is resized (see Figure 4-21).

Set the Anchor property of each control on the main application window to the value shown in Table 4-1.

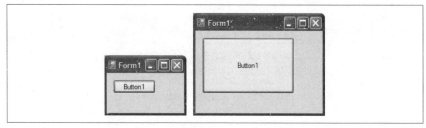

Figure 4-21. Setting the Anchor property of a control to "Top, Bottom, Left, Right"

Table 4-1. Setting the Anchor property of the various controls

Control name	Value
txtKeywords	Top, Left, Right
btnGetInfo	Top, Right
lstBooks	Top, Bottom, Left, Right
chkAutoAdd	Bottom, Left, Right
chkShowCover	Bottom, Left, Right
btnViewCatalog	Bottom, Left, Right
lblISBN	Top, Left
txtTitle	Top, Left, Right
txtAuthors	Top, Left, Right
txtPublisher	Top, Left, Right
txtPrice	Top, Left, Right
picCover	Top, Right
btnAddTitle	Bottom, Left

While you're at it, also set the properties of three other controls on the window to the values shown in Table 4-2.

Table 4-2. Setting the properties of the various controls

Control name	Property	Value	Description
lblISBN	BorderStyle	FixedSingle	This draws a rectangle around the control.
chkShowCover	Checked	True	The control is checked by default.
picCover	SizeMode	AutoSize	The image will be displayed in its original size.

The resizing and reallocating of controls is much improved in VB 2005 compared to VB 6. By setting the Anchor property of each control, you can ensure that the controls are automatically resized or repositioned when the user resizes the form, as shown in Figure 4-22.

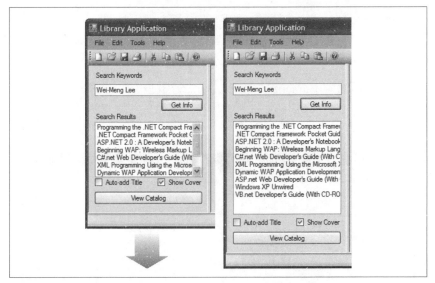

Figure 4-22. Resizing the controls

Adding a Web Reference to Amazon.com

The Library Application uses Amazon.com's E-Commerce web service (ECS for short) to obtain detailed information about a book, such as its description, selling price, customers' reviews, and cover image. To use the Amazon.com web service, you need to register as a user and use the subscription ID assigned to you by Amazon to access the service programmatically. You can register for the service at: *www.amazon.com/gp/aws/landing.html*. There is no charge for using the service. To continue with this example, you should register now.

Once you have registered with Amazon.com, you need to add a web reference to your project to use the service. Once you have added the web reference, Visual Studio 2005 can automatically generate a proxy class for you so that you can invoke the web service as if you were making calls to a normal object, as you will see in the next section, "Accessing the Amazon.com Web Services."

1. To add a web reference to your project, right-click on the project name in Solution Explorer and then select Add Web Reference.

2. In the Add Web Reference window, enter the following URL and click Go: *http://webservices.amazon.com/AWSECommerceService/AWSECommerceService.wsdl.*

This URL contains the location of the WSDL document needed by Visual Studio 2005 to generate the web proxy class.

3. If the WSDL document is retrieved successfully, you can add it to your project by clicking the Add Reference button (see Figure 4-23). Name the web reference *AmazonWS*.

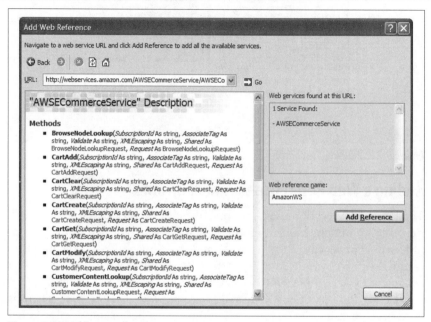

Figure 4-23. Adding a web reference

Accessing the Amazon.com Web Services

When a Library Application user enters search keywords for a book, the application needs to connect to Amazon.com's web service to request a search and download the list of titles returned. While the user waits for the result, it's always a good idea to report the status of the search in the StatusStrip control with some text as well as an hourglass cursor, as shown in Figure 4-24.

In this section, you'll first program the controls that show status. You'll use the StatusLabel control on Form1 to display some status text while the search proceeds and change the cursor to an hourglass to provide a visual representation of work in progress. Once the status controls are coded, you'll write

Web Services

A web service is a business object residing on a server that you can programmatically access through the network. For example, companies like Amazon.com and Google have both found values in making parts of their data available to their customers through web services. Using web services, customers can now integrate data from Amazon.com or Google into their own application. To ensure interoperability between web services and their users (known as *web service consumers*), most web services use open standards such as SOAP, XML, HTTP, and WSDL:

XML
  Used as the language for exchanging messages between a web service and its consumer.

SOAP (Simple Object Access Protocol)
  Used as the XML messaging format.

HTTP
  Used as the transport protocol to carry web services messages.

WSDL (Web Services Description Language)
  Used to write the contract that defines the functions that the web service has to offer.

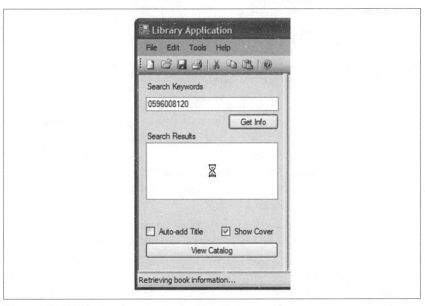

Figure 4-24. Displaying the status in the StatusStrip control

the code that calls the Amazon.com web service and loads information retrieved by the keyword search into the ListBox control (lstBooks) that displays the result.

1. You will first define two global variables within the form to use the Amazon.com web service:

```
Public Class Form1
    '---objects to store the response of the Web service
    Dim amazonResponse As AmazonWS.ItemSearchResponse = Nothing
    Dim amazonItems As AmazonWS.Item( ) = Nothing
```

 Note the parentheses ( ) after Item, which are required.

2. To code the status control and change the default cursor to the hourglass, double-click on the Get Info button (btnGetInfo) to switch to the code behind for its Click event handler. Enter the code shown in Example 4-1.

Example 4-1. btnGetInfo Click event handler

```
Private Sub btnGetInfo_Click( _
    ByVal sender As System.Object, _
    ByVal e As System.EventArgs) _
    Handles btnGetInfo.Click

    '---changes the cursor to an hourglass
    Me.Cursor = Cursors.WaitCursor
    ToolStripStatusLabel1.Text = "Retrieving book information..."
    GetBookInformation(Trim(txtKeywords.Text))
End Sub
```

The code in Example 4-1 displays status text (by setting the Text property of ToolStripStatusLabel1) and changes the default cursor to use an hourglass (using the Me.Cursor property). Next, the event handler calls GetBookInformation, which calls the Amazon.com event handler and passes it the search keywords that the user has entered into the txtKeyword text box control.

3. Now you need to code the GetBookInformation subroutine. The GetBookInformation subroutine takes a single parameter (keyword) and calls the Amazon.com web service. When the result is returned, display it in the Search Results window of the Library Application. Figure 4-25 shows the results you'll get when you enter my name as the search string.

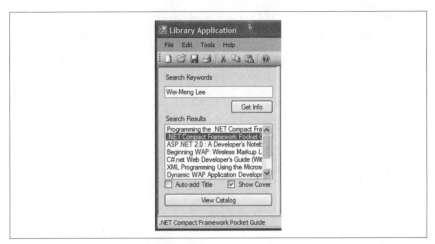

Figure 4-25. Displaying the results from Amazon.com

Add the GetBookInformation subroutine to the Form1 class on its code-behind page by entering the code shown in Example 4-2. Remember to assign the value of the subscription ID assigned you by Amazon.com to SubscriptionId.

Example 4-2. GetBookInformation subroutine

```
Public Sub GetBookInformation(ByVal keyword As String)
    Dim itemSearchRequest As New AmazonWS.ItemSearchRequest
    Dim itemSearch As New AmazonWS.ItemSearch
    '---initialize objects
    With itemSearchRequest
        '---set the search keyword(s)
        .Keywords = keyword

        '---set the size of the response
        .ResponseGroup = New String() {"Medium"}

        '---set the SearchIndex or search mode
        .SearchIndex = "Books"
    End With

    With itemSearch
        '---set the Amazon.com SubscriptionId
        .SubscriptionId = "your_subscription_Id_here"
        .Request = New AmazonWS.ItemSearchRequest() _
            {itemSearchRequest}
    End With

    Try
        '---invoke the Amazon.com web service
        amazonResponse = _
```

Example 4-2. GetBookInformation subroutine (continued)

```
            My.WebServices.AWSECommerceService.ItemSearch(itemSearch)

        If amazonResponse IsNot Nothing Then
            amazonItems = amazonResponse.Items(0).Item
        End If
    Catch ex as Exception
        MsgBox(ex.ToString)
    Finally
        '---change the cursor to default
        Me.Cursor = Cursors.Default
        ToolStripStatusLabel1.Text = ""
    End Try

    If amazonItems Is Nothing then Exit Sub

    lstBooks.Items.Clear()
    '---add the books to the listbox
    For i As Integer = 0 To amazonItems.Length - 1
        With amazonItems(i)
            lstBooks.Items.Add(.ItemAttributes.Title)
        End With
    Next
End Sub
```

 For simplicity, the Library Application will retrieve only the first 10 results from Amazon.com.

Displaying Book Information and Covers

With the results of a search now available in the Search Results window, you want to enable users to view the details of any title in the list by selecting its name.

When a title is selected, a number of actions need to occur. First, the application needs to display the book details in the righthand pane of the Library Application window. Book covers require special handling. Since most users will want to see the cover of a book they've chosen, the Show Cover checkbox in Figure 4-24 is set to True (checked) by default. Unless the user unchecks the box, the cover of a title is always retrieved along with its other information. However, the Amazon.com web service supplies a URL that points to the location of the image, not the image itself. So, you'll need to write code to download the image onto the local computer before you can display it.

Finally, if the user has checked the Auto-add Title checkbox, the application needs to automatically add the selected title to the database.

Abiding by the Amazon Web Services Licenses Agreement

The Amazon Web Services Licenses Agreement describes the set of rules and time limits that you must respect to remain compliant with the license. In particular, applications that store data in a database must store a timestamp along with the data, show this timestamp adjacent to the data, and offer a Refresh function.

The actions can all be carried out by the event handler for the SelectedIndexChanged event of the lstBook listbox control, which fires when a user clicks on any item in its list.

1. To generate a code stub for the SelectedIndexChanged event of the lstBook control, double-click on the control on Form1. To code the event, enter the code shown in bold in Example 4-3.

Example 4-3. lstBooks SelectedIndexChanged event handler

```
Private Sub lstBooks_SelectedIndexChanged( _
    ByVal sender As System.Object, _
    ByVal e As System.EventArgs) _
    Handles lstBooks.SelectedIndexChanged

    If lstBooks.SelectedIndex < 0 Then Exit Sub

    Try
        '---display detailed book information
        With amazonItems(lstBooks.SelectedIndex)
            lblISBN.Text = .ASIN
            txtTitle.Text = .ItemAttributes.Title
            txtAuthors.Text = Join(.ItemAttributes.Author, ",")
            txtPublisher.Text = .ItemAttributes.Publisher
            txtPrice.Text = _
                .ItemAttributes.ListPrice.FormattedPrice.ToString
            ToolStripStatusLabel1.Text = .ItemAttributes.Title

            '---downloads the cover of the book
            If chkShowCover.Checked Then
                '---download the cover image
                Dim webReq As Net.HttpWebRequest = _
                    Net.HttpWebRequest.Create( _
                        .MediumImage.URL.ToString)
                Dim webResp As Net.HttpWebResponse = _
                    webReq.GetResponse( )

                '---displays the image
                picCover.Image = _
                    Image.FromStream(webResp.GetResponseStream( ))
```

Example 4-3. lstBooks SelectedIndexChanged event handler (continued)

```
        End If

            '---auto-add a title
            If chkAutoAdd.Checked Then
                AddTitle( )
            End If
        End With
    Catch ex As Exception
        DisplayError(ex.ToString)
    End Try
End Sub
```

2. The `DisplayError` method that you call in Example 4-4 simply sounds a beep and displays the error message in the `StatusLabel` control in the `StatusStrip` control.

Example 4-4. DisplayError subroutine

```
Private Sub DisplayError(ByVal message As String)
    My.Computer.Audio.PlaySystemSound( _
        System.Media.SystemSounds.Exclamation)
    ToolStripStatusLabel1.Text = "Error : " & message
End Sub
```

You can play different types of sounds by supplying the `PlaySystemSound` method with one of the following values from the `System.Media.SystemSounds` enumeration:

- `Asterisk`
- `Beep`
- `Exclamation`
- `Hand`
- `Question`

Figure 4-25, earlier in this chapter, shows the result of a search for the author Wei-Meng Lee. When you click on the title of one of the books in the results list (for example, *ASP.NET 2.0: A Developer's Notebook*), the detailed information available for the selected book is displayed.

Saving Book Information

Now you need to write the routines that add book information to the user's database either because "Auto-add Title box" is checked or because the user has clicked the Add Title button. While the detailed book information about a title is displayed on the form, you'll also want to give the user the option to modify the data before saving it to the local database file.

1. First, you'll code the Add Title button event handler. Double-click the Add Title button on Form1 and enter the code in Example 4-5.

Example 4-5. btnAddTitle Click event handler

```
Private Sub btnAddTitle_Click( _
   ByVal sender As System.Object, _
   ByVal e As System.EventArgs) _
   Handles btnAddTitle.Click
   AddTitle( )
End Sub
```

The event handler calls the AddTitle subroutine, where the heavy lifting is done.

2. The AddTitle subroutine called by Example 4-6 is responsible for recording the details of a title you want stored in the local database file, *Library.mdf*. The subroutine first converts the image displayed in the PictureBox control into a byte array. The new record is then saved into the database using the TitlesTableAdapter control that you added to the form earlier (see also Figure 4-17, earlier in this chapter).

Example 4-6. AddTitle subroutine

```
Public Sub AddTitle( )
    Try
        '---get the book cover image as a byte array---
        Dim ms As New System.IO.MemoryStream( )
        picCover.Image.Save(ms, picCover.Image.RawFormat)
        Dim coverimage( ) As Byte = ms.GetBuffer
        ms.Close( )

        '---add the new title to the database---
        TitlesTableAdapter.Insert(lblISBN.Text, _
            txtTitle.Text, txtAuthors.Text, _
            txtPublisher.Text, txtPrice.Text, coverimage)
        ToolStripStatusLabel1.Text += " - Added"
    Catch ex As Exception
        DisplayError("Error adding title.")
    End Try
End Sub
```

 All the hard work needed to save the new record into the database is performed by the TitlesTableAdapter control. The TitlesTableAdapter control uses ADO.NET (the data access technology used in the .NET Framework) behind the scenes to accomplish this mean feat.

Testing the Application

Now you are ready to take the application for a test drive. Start it up by pressing F5. Enter some keywords for a book, say, the author name, title, or ISBN. Click on the Get Info button to retrieve a list of titles matching your search criteria and list them on the Listbox control. You'll notice that the application hangs for a while when you submit the search request, and the form does not appear to repaint itself when overlapped by another window. We'll deal with this problem in a future section, "Accessing the Web Services Asynchronously." You can display the details of a book in the right-hand pane of the application window by selecting an item in the ListBox control of the Search Results window, as shown in Figure 4-26.

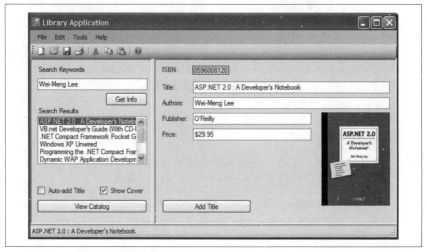

Figure 4-26. Testing the application

Click the Add Title button to save the book information into the local database. If you check the "Auto-add Title" checkbox, book information is saved automatically just by selecting a title from the Search Results list.

 If you were to include similar functionality in a production application, you would need to store the "freshness date" along with each book, display that date along with the other information, and offer the user the ability to refresh the data to make sure the price and other information is accurate. See the Amazon license agreement for details.

Viewing Book Information Offline

With the book information saved in the database, you will now add a second window to the project so that users can view their book catalogs offline. The Books Catalog window will be invoked by clicking on the View Catalog button that you've already added to the Library Application main window. By clicking on any title listed in the catalog, the user will be able to display its details, including an image of its cover.

You'll build the Books Catalog window using the new Data Source Configuration Wizard and two new controls: DataGridView and BindingNavigator. With the exception of the event handler for the View Catalog button, you'll accomplish this task without writing any code.

Create the Books Catalog Window

First you need to create the window that will display the book catalog and make it accessible from the Library Application main window.

1. To create the Books Catalog page, add another form to the project by right-clicking on the project name, *LibraryApp*, in Solution Explorer and then selecting Add → New Item… Select the Windows Form template and use the default name *Form2.vb*. Click Add and note the addition of the form to the *LibraryApp* project in the Solution Explorer.

2. Set the Text property of *Form2.vb* to "Books Catalog," which changes the title of the form to "Books Catalog." Now the title reflects the purpose of the form in the application.

3. Finally, you need to link the Books Catalog page to the main application window. On the *Form1.vb* design page, double-click on the View Catalog button and enter the single bold line of code in Example 4-7.

Example 4-7. btnViewCatalog Click event handler

```
Private Sub btnViewCatalog_Click( _
   ByVal sender As System.Object, _
   ByVal e As System.EventArgs) _
   Handles btnViewCatalog.Click
   Form2.ShowDialog( )
End Sub
```

When a user clicks the View Catalog button, the Books Catalog page (*Form2.vb*) will be displayed.

Binding Library Data to the Books Catalog Form

You will once again use the data-binding features of VB 2005 to display all the records in the database on the newly added form.

1. Go to Data → Show Data Sources to display the Data Sources window.

2. Change the binding of the *Titles* table to the DataGridView control (see Figure 4-27).

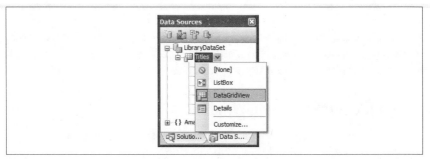

Figure 4-27. Binding the Titles table to a DataGridView control

3. Drag-and-drop the *Titles* table from the Data Sources window onto *Form2.vb*. A DataGridView and a BindingNavigator control will be created automatically. In the DataGridView Tasks menu, check the Enable Column Reordering checkbox so that users can sort the rows of their catalog entries by field. The DataGridView Tasks menu is shown in Figure 4-28.

Figure 4-28. Configuring the DataGridView control

4. Since the list of titles shown in the Books Catalog window doesn't have to include everything there is to know about each book, it makes sense to display the *Title*, *Authors*, and *Publisher* fields only. To remove the unwanted fields, go to the `DataGridView` Tasks menu again, click on the Edit Columns link, and remove the following fields:

   - *ISBN*
   - *Price*
   - *Cover*

   The result is a list of books that displays only the title, authors, and the publisher.

5. You will now change the binding of the *Titles* table in the Data Sources window from `DataGridView` to `Details`. This will allow you to display individual records instead of multiple records on the form.

   Now drag-and-drop the *Titles* table from the Data Sources window onto *Form2.vb*.

6. Finally, you'll want to add a Close button to the Books Catalog window so users can close the form when they've finished using it. To do that, add a `Button` control to *Form2.vb* and set its `Text` property to "Close." Name the `Button` control btnClose. *Form2.vb* will now look like the version shown in Figure 4-29.

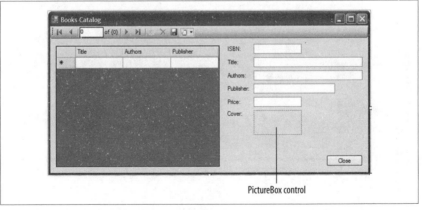

Figure 4-29. Form2 with the various controls

7. To wire up the `Click` event handler for the Close button, double-click on the Close button and enter the code shown in Example 4-8. It's worth noting that this is the only code you've had to write to create this form.

Example 4-8. Close button Click event handler

```
Private Sub btnClose_Click( _
    ByVal sender As System.Object, _
    ByVal e As System.EventArgs) _
    Handles btnClose.Click
     ' Me refers to the current object (Form2)
    Me.Close()
End Sub
```

8. One last step remains. On Form2, set the PictureBox control's SizeMode property to AutoSize so that the cover of a book can be displayed in its original downloaded size.

Testing the Application

You can now test the application by pressing F5. On *Form1.vb*, click on the View Catalog button to display *Form2.vb*, as shown in Figure 4-30.

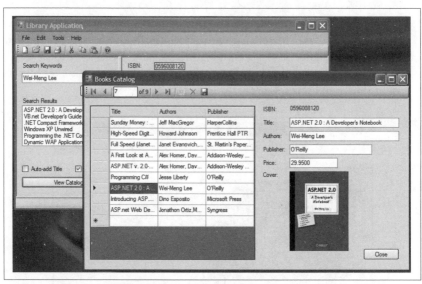

Figure 4-30. Displaying the catalog of books

Try editing existing records by modifying the data in the DataGridView control or the text boxes on the right of the window. To save changes to the database, you need to click the Save Data button, as shown in Figure 4-31. You can also delete records by clicking on the Delete button and then the Save Data button to effect the change.

Note that for simplicity, you will not be able to add new records in this window as the *ISBN* field is non-editable.

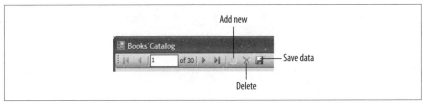

Figure 4-31. Adding and deleting records

Deploying the Application

Visual Studio 2005 makes the deployment of Windows applications to your users extremely easy and painless, all through a new feature known as *Click-Once*.

Smart Clients

ClickOnce was designed specifically to ease the deployment of smart clients.

A *smart client* is basically a Windows application that leverages the system's local resources and is able to intelligently connect to distributed data sources (such as web services) as and when needed.

The Library Application that you've been building in this chapter is an example of a smart client. While today a lot of companies are deploying web applications (due to their ubiquitous access), network latencies and server delays are some of the problems that are preventing developers from reaping the full benefits of the Web. Common frustrations over web applications include slow response time from web sites and limited functionality (due to the stateless nature of the HTTP protocol). As such, a smart client aims to reap the benefit of the rich functionality of the client (Windows) while at the same time using the power of web services in the backend.

To illustrate how ClickOnce works, you will publish the Library Application (LibraryApp) that you have written and see how easy it is to deploy it using a web server. Furthermore, ClickOnce has the added benefit of ensuring that applications that you deploy will automatically check for the latest update (you can configure the application to check every time before it runs, or check at regular time intervals) on the server, if one is available, as you'll see in "Automatic Updating," later in this capter.

Publishing the Application

You can now publish (deploy) a Windows application through a disk, shared folder, FTP server, or web server, and automatically ensure that users are always using the latest version of the application.

1. To run the ClickOnce Publish Wizard, go to Build → Publish LibraryApp on the Visual Studio menu, as shown in Figure 4-32. The "Where do you want to publish" dialog box will appear.

Figure 4-32. Publishing the LibraryApp Windows application

2. The "Where do you want to publish" dialog box gives you four options for where to publish the application: disk, shared folder, FTP server, or web server. For this project, you will publish the application through the IIS web server (see the sidebar "Installing IIS on Your Computer" on how to install IIS on your Windows XP computer).

Installing IIS on Your Computer

If you wish to use IIS to deploy your Windows applications, you must install IIS. By default, Windows XP does not install IIS, so you need to retrieve your Windows XP Installation CD and then use Control Panel → Add or Remove Programs → Add/Remove Windows Components → Components: Internet Information Services (IIS) to add IIS yourself.

In the "Specify the location to publish the application" text box, create a directory for the application by entering the following link: *http:// localhost/LibraryApp* (see Figure 4-33). Click Next. The "Will the application be available offline?" dialog will appear.

Localhost is the name of the web server installed in your local computer.

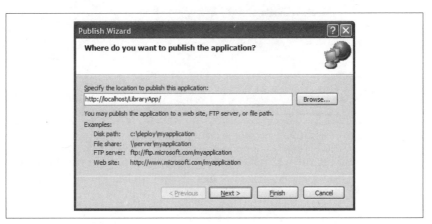

Figure 4-33. Specifying the path to publish the folder

3. ClickOnce allows the user to install an application locally on the client, or to download every time it is needed. In the "Will the application be available offline?" dialog, select "Yes," as shown in Figure 4-34, and then click Next. The "Ready to Publish!" dialog will appear.

Figure 4-34. Choosing the mode in which the application should be run

4. That's it! You are now ready to publish the application from your web server. In the "Ready to Publish!" dialog shown in Figure 4-35, click Finish to create the web page that users will link to in order to install the application.

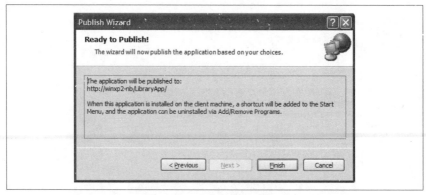

Figure 4-35. The wizard is ready to publish the application

5. You should see the web page shown in Figure 4-36. Your users can now use the URL for that page to install the application on their own machines.

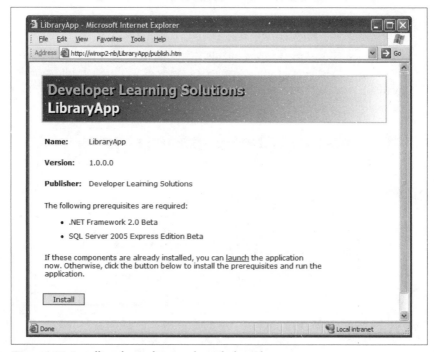

Figure 4-36. Installing the application through the web server

6. To install the application on your own machine, click the *launch* link in the page.

 Click the Install button to install the prerequisites, if your machine does not have them.

7. You will be prompted with a security warning such as the one shown in Figure 4-37. Click Install to install the application onto your machine.

 You can eliminate this security warning by setting the relevant security policy. Refer to the MSDN Help Topic "Code Access Security for ClickOnce Applications" for more information. Also, check out the help topic "How to: Sign Click-Once Application and Deployment Manifests" (*http://msdn2. microsoft.com/library/che5h906(en-us,vs.80).aspx*) for more information.

Figure 4-37. Installing the application

8. You will now see that the *LibraryApp* application is launched automatically. Alternatively, you can launch the LibraryApp application from Start → Programs → LibraryApp → LibraryApp.

 The ClickOnce installation does not require you to have administrator rights to install the application.

Automatic Updating

The power of ClickOnce lies in its ability to automatically update applications after they have been deployed. Imagine that 1000 of your customers have downloaded your application and that you've decided you need to add some new features or fix a fatal bug. With VB 6, it would be a logistical nightmare to inform all these customers of the changes and then to update their machines. ClickOnce automatically ensures that all your users use the latest version of your application.

To demonstrate the power of ClickOnce, you'll make a useful change to the Library Application—and learn something about the new BackgroundWorker control in the process—and then use the automatic update feature of Click-Once to get the new version into the hands of your users.

> The BackgroundWorker control is a control that executes an operation on a separate thread.

Accessing the Web Services Asynchronously

In testing the Library Application in an earlier section (see "Testing the Application), you saw that the application freezes when you request and download keyword search results from Amazon.com. Moreover, the window does not repaint itself when it is covered by some other windows. So, what is the problem? It turns out that accessing a web service is a *blocking call*, which means that the application will not continue its execution until the web service returns a value. In the real world, web services requests take a finite amount of time to complete and hence it is not acceptable that our application freezes while waiting for the results from Amazon.com.

To make the UI of your application responsive, you need to invoke the web service call in a separate *thread* of execution.

While this may sound intimidating (see the sidebar "VB Black Belt: Multi-threading" for more information on threading), VB 2005 has made it easy to add this functionality to an application by providing a new BackgroundWorker control. To see how the BackgroundWorker control helps make your application more responsive, you will use it to access the Amazon.com web service in the background, and while so doing, the application can remain active. Here is a summary of the steps involved:

VB Black Belt: Multithreading

Multithreading is one of the most powerful concepts in programming. Using multithreading, you can break a complex task into multiple threads that execute independently of one another. One particularly good application of multithreading is in tasks that are synchronous in nature, such as web services calls. By default, web services calls are blocking calls; that is, the caller code will not continue until the web service returns a result. But because web services calls are often slow, this can result in sluggish client-side performance unless you take special steps to make the call asynchronous.

By default, your Windows application uses a single thread of execution. In our project, we have created an additional thread of execution to access the web service.

One particular point you need to bear in mind is that Windows controls are not thread-safe. Put simply, it means that you cannot update the properties of a Windows control in a separate thread; only the main thread can update the controls.

1. The user clicks the Get Info button, and the BackgroundWorker control kicks into action.

2. The BackgroundWorker control runs the GetBookInformation subroutine (which is defined by you) in a separate thread, with the main window remaining responsive.

3. When the result is returned from Amazon.com, the BackgroundWorker control updates the controls on the window with the detailed book information.

Here are the steps:

1. First, you need to add the BackgroundWorker control to your application. Drag-and-drop the control from the Components tab in the Toolbox onto *Form1.vb* of the *LibraryApp* project. Because the BackgroundWorker control is not a visual control, you will see its icon at the bottom of the form, as shown in Figure 4-38.

Figure 4-38. Using the BackgroundWorker control

2. Switch to the code-behind page of Form1 and import the System.ComponentModel namespace—which is needed in order to use the classes that the BackgroundWorker control needs to do its work—by adding the following line of code (in bold) to the top of the code behind of *Form1.vb*.

```
Imports System.ComponentModel
Public Class Form1
    ...
```

3. When the Get Info button is clicked, you will use the BackgroundWorker control to call the web service in a separate thread using its RunWorkerAsync method, which starts the execution of a background operation. The method takes a single parameter, which in this case is the keyword(s) that the user has entered. To replace the current Click event handler for the Get Info button, double-click on the control on Form1 and replace the existing code with that in Example 4-9.

Example 4-9. Revised code for btn Click event handler

```
Private Sub btnGetInfo_Click( _
    ByVal sender As System.Object, _
    ByVal e As System.EventArgs) _
    Handles btnGetInfo.Click

    '---retrieve the book info in the background
    BackgroundWorker1.RunWorkerAsync( _
        Trim(txtKeywords.Text))

    '---changes the cursor to an hourglass
    Me.Cursor = Cursors.WaitCursor
    ToolStripStatusLabel1.Text = _
        "Retrieving book information..."

End Sub
```

4. The DoWork event of the BackgroundWorker control will invoke GetBookInformation subroutine in a separate thread. The DoWork event is fired when you call the RunWorkerAsync method, as you did in the previous step. The argument passed to the RunWorkerAsync method can be retrieved in the DoWork event via the System.ComponentModel.DoWorkEventArgs parameter. Add the event shown in Example 4-10 to the Form1 class.

Example 4-10. BackgroundWorker DoWork event handler

```
Private Sub BackgroundWorker1_DoWork( _
    ByVal sender As System.Object, _
    ByVal e As System.ComponentModel.DoWorkEventArgs) _
    Handles BackgroundWorker1.DoWork
    'This method will run on a thread other than the UI thread.
```

Example 4-10. BackgroundWorker DoWork event handler (continued)

```
'Be sure not to manipulate any Windows Forms controls created
'on the UI thread from this method.

Dim worker As BackgroundWorker = _
    CType(sender, BackgroundWorker)
GetBookInformation(e.Argument, worker, e)
End Sub
```

5. The GetBookInformation subroutine accesses the Amazon.com web service. Replace the GetBookInformation subroutine you have defined earlier with that shown in Example 4-11.

Example 4-11. Revised GetBookInformation subroutine

```
Public Sub GetBookInformation( _
    ByVal keyword As String, _
    ByVal worker As BackgroundWorker, _
    ByVal e As DoWorkEventArgs)

    Dim itemSearchRequest As New AmazonWS.ItemSearchRequest
    Dim itemSearch As New AmazonWS.ItemSearch

    '---initialize objects
    With itemSearchRequest
        '---set the search keyword(s)
        .Keywords = keyword

        '---set the size of the response
        .ResponseGroup = New String() {"Medium"}

        '---set the SearchIndex or search mode
        .SearchIndex = "Books"
    End With

    With itemSearch
        '---set the Amazon.com SubscriptionId
        .SubscriptionId = "your_subscription_Id_here"
        .Request = New AmazonWS.ItemSearchRequest() {itemSearchRequest}
    End With

    Try
        '---invoke the Amazon.com web service
        amazonResponse = _
            My.WebServices.AWSECommerceService.ItemSearch(itemSearch)

        If amazonResponse IsNot Nothing Then
            amazonItems = amazonResponse.Items(0).Item
        End If
    Catch ex as Exception
        '---an error has occured
    End Try
End Sub
```

Notice that in this subroutine, you need not worry about displaying the returned result in the Listbox control; you will do that in the next step.

6. The RunWorkerCompleted event is fired when the thread (in this case, GetBookInformation) is completed. In Example 4-12, you will get the result returned from the web service and then add the items into the Listbox control.

Example 4-12. BackgroundWorker1_RunWorkerCompleted event handler

```
Private Sub BackgroundWorker1_RunWorkerCompleted( _
    ByVal sender As Object, _
    ByVal e As System.ComponentModel.RunWorkerCompletedEventArgs) _
    Handles BackgroundWorker1.RunWorkerCompleted

    '--change to cursor to default
    Me.Cursor = Cursors.Default
    ToolStripStatusLabel1.Text = ""

    If Not (e.Error Is Nothing) Then
        MessageBox.Show(e.Error.Message)
    Else
        If amazonItems Is Nothing then Exit Sub
        lstBooks.Items.Clear()
        '---add the books to the listbox
        For i As Integer = 0 To amazonItems.Length - 1
            With amazonItems(i)
                lstBooks.Items.Add(.ItemAttributes.Title)
            End With
        Next
    End If
End Sub
```

That's it! You can now debug the application by pressing F5. You should find the UI of the application is still responsive while waiting for the result from the Amazon.com web service.

Republishing the Application

Now that you have modified your *LibraryApp* application, you should rebuild it and republish it so that users can be automatically updated through ClickOnce.

1. Rebuild the project by right-clicking on the project name (*LibraryApp*) in Solution Explorer and selecting Rebuild.

2. To ensure that your users can use the updated application, build and publish the application again, following the steps outlined earlier. That's all you need to do.

3. The next time your users launch the application from the Start menu, the application will automatically check the deployment server to see if there is a newer version available. If there is one, the Update Available window will be displayed (see Figure 4-39). Click OK to download, install, and use the newer version of the application.

 A network connection is needed for auto-updating to work. The auto-updating is configurable. You could set it to check at some regular interval as well, specified in minutes, hours, or days.

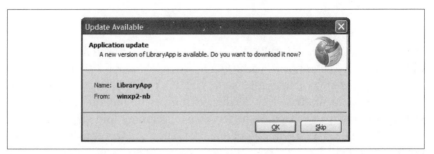

Figure 4-39. Downloading a newer version of the StockQuote application

4. What happens if, after installing the newer version, you decide that you want to use the older version? No worries; just go to Control Panel and click Add or Remove Programs, select the application, and click Change/Remove. You have the option to either restore the application to its previous state or remove the application.

Summary

In this chapter, you have seen how easily Visual Studio 2005 and the VB 2005 language can be used to create professional applications. In particular, you have seen how to create a database and bind its records to a data access form; how web services can be consumed in a Visual Studio 2005 project; and how data can be persisted in a SQL database for offline perusal. You have also learned how ClickOnce makes deployment and updating of smart clients easy and effortless and how you can painlessly add asynchronous calls to an application.

In the next chapter, you will learn how to use VB 2005 to develop web applications.

CHAPTER 5
Building Web Applications

Within a short few years, ASP.NET has become a favorite tool of web applications developers and now, with the release of ASP.NET 2.0, it has undergone its second major upgrade. With ASP.NET 2.0, Microsoft has made major improvements based on feedback from its millions of customers as well as the company's own experience in developing and deploying web sites and portals. The rise of competing tools such as Macromedia Flash and open source PHP have also encouraged Microsoft to focus with particular intensity on improving the ease of use of ASP.NET while reducing the amount of code developers must write to create web applications.

For the Visual Basic 2005 programmer, the new release of ASP.NET is yet another bonanza, making web application development more accessible then ever to those with Visual Basic skills. Among its many improvements, ASP.NET 2.0 ships with dozens of new ready-to-use controls, considerably reducing the amount of code you need to write to achieve professional results. In fact, a stated aim of the Microsoft web development tools team is to reduce the amount of code you write to perform common web site tasks by up to 70%. In addition, ASP.NET 2.0 comes with some neat improvements, such as cross-page posting and the ability to insert client script into a page. You will learn about some of these features in this chapter.

The new features in ASP.NET 2.0 can be grouped into three broad categories: new controls and control functionality, improvements to the Page Framework, and new services and APIs.

Controls
   ASP.NET 2.0 ships with more than 50 new controls that make the life of a web application developer easier by eliminating the need to write code. Specifically, there are new controls that help you to perform data access, site navigation, login, and personalization with Web Parts.

Page Framework

ASP.NET 2.0 supports some useful additions to its Page Framework, most importantly establishing a common look and feel on a site through a feature known as Master Pages. In addition to Master Pages, ASP.NET 2.0 supports "theming" through Themes and Skins, allowing you to maintain a consistent look and feel for your web sites and their controls. Another noteworthy feature in ASP.NET is its improved support for localization, which reduces the amount of work you need to do to internationalize your web applications.

Services and APIs

Behind the various new ASP.NET 2.0 controls for web site development lie the foundation services and APIs that do the heavy lifting the controls need to do their work. For example, behind the new Login controls you'll find the new Membership APIs, which perform such tasks as user authentication, registration of new users, etc. If the controls don't do what you need, you can make use of these APIs directly in code.

In this chapter, you will build a simple e-commerce web application using several of the most powerful and interesting features of Visual Studio 2005 and ASP.NET 2.0. The site will enable users—whether or not they are authenticated—to browse a list of books and add one or more to a shopping cart. Once a user is ready to checkout, the site will display a page asking the user either to log in or register as a new member and then proceed to log in as a new member.

As you build the site, you'll get a feel for the following Visual Studio 2005 and ASP.NET 2.0 features:

- How to create a consistent look and feel for your web site using Master Pages
- How to use the new Profiling services to save items into a shopping cart and keep track of them when a user registers and logs into the site
- How to use the new security controls to create user accounts and to authenticate users
- How to use new Member services to create a members-only directory of pages
- How to display data using the GridView control

Of course, since this is a Visual Basic 2005 book, you'll also get to write some code. Figure 5-1 shows how the main page of application will look when it is completed. Users will click on the Add to Cart buttons to add items to their shopping cart and click on the Checkout button to go to the login page to sign in and make a purchase.

Figure 5-1. The completed shopping cart application

Building the Storefront

The first step toward building the example in this chapter is to create the Storefront page shown in Figure 5-1. You'll first create a Master Page to set the look and feel of the site and then derive the Storefront page from it. Once the page is created, you'll add the controls needed to define its buttons and to display the books. To get started, you'll use Visual Studio 2005 to create a new Visual Basic web application.

1. On the Visual Studio menu bar, click File → New Web Site..., as shown in Figure 5-2. The New Web Site dialog box will display.

2. In the New Web Site dialog, select the ASP.NET Web Site template. Select File System as its Location, and Visual Basic as the Language you will use. Name the project *C:\ShoppingApp*. Figure 5-3 shows the result. Click OK to continue. Visual Studio 2005 will create the site and display its files in the Solution Explorer. Take a look at the toolbar, which

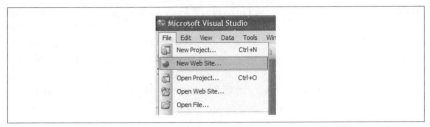

Figure 5-2. Using Visual Studio 2005 for this project

lists an entirely different set of controls specifically provided for building web applications. You'll be using a number of these later in the chapter.

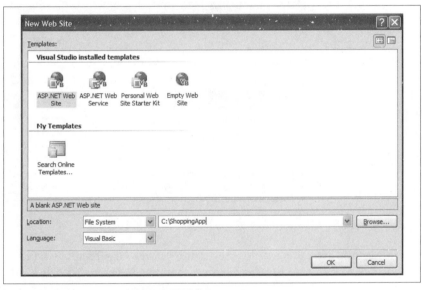

Figure 5-3. Creating a new ASP.NET Web Site project

File-Based Web Development

Visual Studio 2005 provides you with four ways to develop a web site. For this project, you'll use the File System option. This new ASP.NET 2.0 option frees you from having to use IIS (Microsoft Internet Information Server) for development. Instead, Visual Studio 2005 provides its own built-in web server, which it launches when you run/debug the web application.

Now you can even develop ASP.NET 2.0 web applications on your Windows XP Home Edition PC, which does not include IIS.

Building a Site Template Using a Master Page

Visual Studio 2005 and ASP.NET 2.0 now support the creation of special pages known as *Master Pages* that you can use to give a common look and feel to every page on your site. The implementation resembles the visual page inheritance found in Windows Forms, for those who have used that popular framework, though strictly speaking, it is not the same. You can create a single Master Page to specify the common elements shared by all the pages of your site. You then create web pages that draw on content from the Master Page.

For the e-commerce site, you will first create a Master Page to define the header that will appear on every page. The header consists of two images, one showing the O'Reilly company logo and the other displaying the O'Reilly company name.

1. To create the Master Page, right-click on the project name in Solution Explorer and then select Add New Item... (see Figure 5-4).

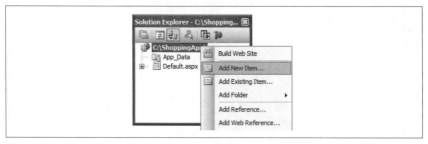

Figure 5-4. Adding a new item to the project

2. In the Add New Item dialog, select the Master Page template and use the default name, *MasterPage.master*, as shown in Figure 5-5. Click Add to create the page.

3. Since you'll be using controls to add elements to the Master Page, go to the *MasterPage.master* page and switch to the Design view by clicking on the Design button at the bottom left of the page, as shown in Figure 5-6.

4. Your project will make use of a number of images, so you need to create a folder to store them. Add a folder to the project and name it *Images* by right-clicking on the project name in Solution Explorer and selecting Add Folder → Regular Folder, as shown in Figure 5-7.

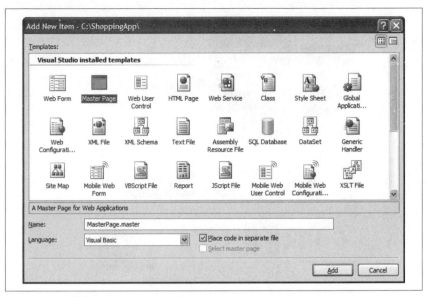

Figure 5-5. Adding a Master Page to the project

Figure 5-6. Switching between Design view and Source view

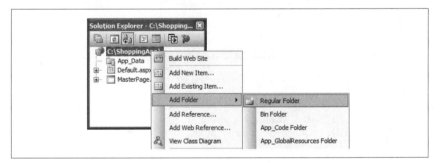

Figure 5-7. Switching between the different views

5. Copy the images shown in Figure 5-8 into the *C:\ShoppingApp\Images* folder. You'll use these images to build your application. When you've finished, the *Images* folder should look like the one shown in Figure 5-9.

The images can be downloaded from this book's support site at *http://www.oreilly.com/catalog/vbjumpstartpg/*.

Figure 5-8. Images used for this project

Figure 5-9. The Images folder with the various images

 You'll need to refresh the *Images* folder to see the images (right-click on the *Images* folder in Solution Explorer and select Refresh Folder).

6. Now you're finally ready to lay out the elements of the Master Page. Drag and drop two Image controls and an HTML Horizontal Rule control from the Toolbox onto the page, as shown in Figure 5-10. Set the names of the controls to those shown in the figure. Make sure the controls are positioned above the ContentPlaceHolder control (simply position your cursor to the left of the ContentPlaceHolder control and press the Enter key a few times to move the control downward).

Switching Between Design View, Source View, and Code-Behind View

In Visual Studio 2005, a Web Form is displayed in Source view by default. Source displays the HTML and other markup a web browser uses to construct a web page you've designed. In Source view, you can directly modify HTML elements and their attributes as well as the controls contained within it. To switch to Design view, click on the Design button at the bottom of the screen. In Design view, you can visually inspect the page and drag and drop controls from the Toolbox onto the form. To view the code behind of the form, you can simply double-click on the form and the code behind will appear. In Code view, you use Visual Basic to write the business logic for your application and service the events raised by the various controls on the page. The figure shows each of the three views.

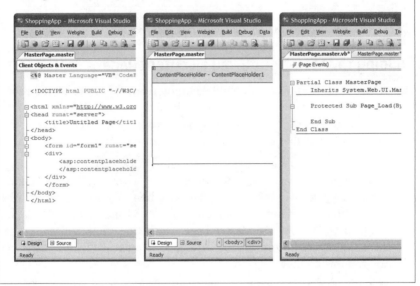

 The ContentPlaceHolder control (populated by default in a Master Page) is a place holder for Content pages (pages that inherit from the Master Page) to populate with controls.

Set the ImageUrl property of the imgLogo control to ~/Images/oreilly_logo.gif and that of the imgHeader control to ~/Images/oreilly_header.gif. The two GIF files contain the O'Reilly company logo and company header, respectively.

7. Save the project (click File → Save All).

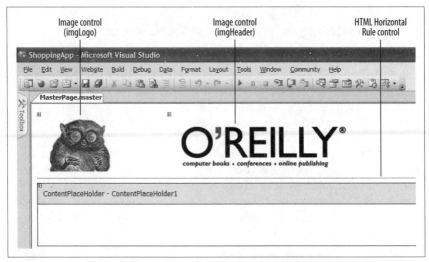

Figure 5-10. Populating the Master Page with the various controls

Building the Storefront Using a Content Page

Now that the Master Page is completed, you're ready to create the Storefront page. You'll do this by deriving (or inheriting) a Content page from the Master Page and then populating it with controls. The Storefront page will display a list of titles that users can add to a shopping cart.

1. To create a blank Content page, right-click on the project name (*ShoppingApp*) in the Solution Explorer and select "Add New Item...." In the Template window of the Add New Item dialog box, select Web Form and set its name to *Main.aspx*. To let Visual Studio 2005 know that you want to use a Master Page, check the "Select master page" checkbox at the bottom of the dialog, as shown in Figure 5-11. Click Add to move to the next step.

2. Now it's time to choose the Master Page. When Visual Studio 2005 displays the Select a Master Page dialog box, select *MasterPage.master* in the Contents of folder pane, as shown in Figure 5-12. Click OK to proceed to the next step.

 Like Visual Basic classes, which can only inherit from one base class, an ASP.NET 2.0 Content page can have only one Master Page.

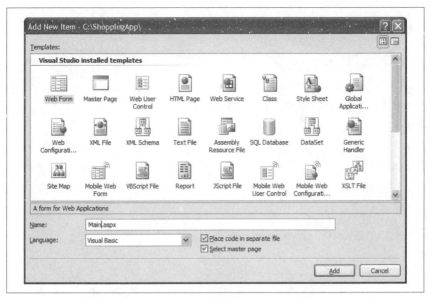

Figure 5-11. Creating a Content page by selecting a Master Page

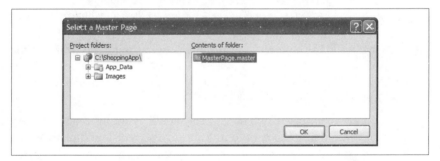

Figure 5-12. Selecting a Master Page

3. Visual Studio 2005 will display the new page, *Main.aspx*, with the contents of the Master Page grayed out, as shown in Figure 5-13. The grayed out sections of the page are meant to indicate that content derived from the Master Page cannot be edited in the *Main.aspx* form. Notice that the new page contains a Content control.

> The Content control is the location where you populate the content of the page.

You'll customize the new page, *Main.aspx*, by adding controls to the Content control in the next step.

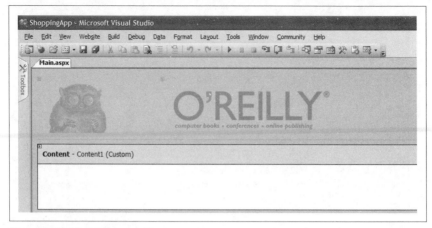

Figure 5-13. Creating a new Content page

While you can't directly edit Master Page content in *Main. aspx*, you can make changes by either right-clicking on the grayed-out content and selecting Edit Master, or by simply going to the Solution Explorer and double-clicking the Master Page. Either action will load the Master Page for editing.

4. Now we'll add the content, specifically the Storefront items available for users to select. Selection in your store will be limited to three items (my O'Reilly books). We'll use a 3 x 2 table to lay out their images and their purchase information.

To add content to a Content control, you'll typically drag-and-drop controls from the Toolbox onto it. You can also type text directly into a Content control if you wish. In the Content control, insert a 3 x 2 table (go to Table → Layout) and then populate the table cells with the controls shown in Figure 5-14. Also, type in the text as shown in the figure. You can drag and drop the detailed information of each book from the following URLs:

- *http://www.oreilly.com/catalog/aspnetadn/*
- *http://www.oreilly.com/catalog/compactframework/*
- *http://www.oreilly.com/catalog/vbjumpstart/*

Set the properties for the controls as follows:

img1

Set the ImageUrl property to ~/Images/aspnetadn.gif.

img2

Set the ImageUrl property to ~/Images/compactframeworkpg.gif.

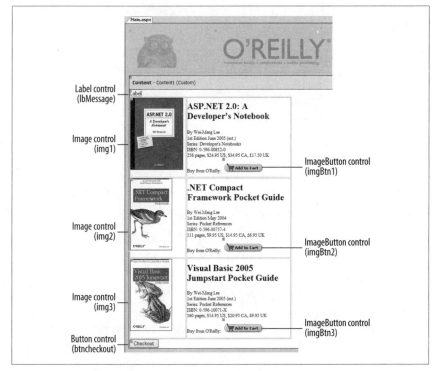

Figure 5-14. Populating the Content page

img3
    Set the ImageUrl property to ~/Images/vbjumpstartpg.gif.

imgBtn1, imgBtn2, imgBtn3
    Set the ImageUrl property to ~/Images/button_addtocart.gif.

Creating a Shopping Cart

When a user clicks on the Add to Cart button on the *Main.aspx* page, you'll want the item to be saved in a shopping cart, a key feature of the application that you'll now implement. To save items, you'll use the new Profile service (exposed via the Profile object) in ASP.NET 2.0. Think of the Profile service as an ASP.NET mechanism to persistently store a user's information, similar to the Session object. Unlike a Profile object, however, a Session object is valid only for the duration of a session; after the session has expired, the Session object is deleted. The Profile service, however, retains its information until you explicitly remove it from the data store.

Moreover, the Profile object has several advantages over the Session object, such as:

Non-volatility
> Profile object data is persisted in data stores, whereas Session variables are saved in memory.

Strong typing
> Profile object properties are strongly typed, unlike Session variables, which are stored as objects and typecast during runtime.

Efficient implementation
> Profile properties are loaded only when they're needed, unlike Session variables, all of which are loaded whenever any one of them is accessed.

In this section, you use the Profile service to implement a shopping cart.

In addition to creating the shopping cart itself, you add forms so that when it comes time to check out, users can either log in to access the members' only area of the site, or register and then log in. You'll use Forms authentication rather than Windows authentication to identify a user.

1. First, you need to create the business object that implements the functionality of a shopping cart. Add a new class to the project and name it *ShoppingCart.vb*. (Right-click on project name in Solution Explorer and select Add New Item.... Then select the Class template and rename it *ShoppingCart.vb*.) You will be asked if you wish to save the file in the *App_Code* folder (see Figure 5-15), which is recommended. Click Yes.

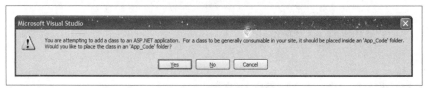

Figure 5-15. Saving the class in the App_Code folder for code reuse

2. Code the *ShoppingCart.vb* class file as shown in Example 5-1.

Example 5-1. ShoppingCart.vb

```
Imports Microsoft.VisualBasic
Imports System.Xml.Serialization

Namespace OReilly

    Public Structure itemType
        Dim isbn As String
        Dim qty As Integer
    End Structure
```

Example 5-1. ShoppingCart.vb (continued)

```
<XmlInclude(GetType(itemType))> _
Public Class Cart
    '---use public for Xml serialization---
    Public items As New _
        System.Collections.Generic.List(Of itemType)

    Public Sub AddItem(ByVal isbn As String, _
                        ByVal qty As Integer)
        Dim cartItem As New itemType
        cartItem.isbn = isbn
        cartItem.qty = qty
        items.Add(cartItem)
    End Sub
End Class
```

```
End Namespace
```

You need to specify the XmlInclude attribute to allow XmlSerializer to recognize a type when it serializes or deserializes the itemType data type.

An item is represented using the itemType structure containing its ISBN number as well as the quantity. The Cart class contains an AddItem method that adds items to a generic List object (located in the System. Collections.Generic namespace). Notice that you use the OReilly namespace to uniquely identify the itemType structure and Cart class that you have defined in this file.

3. Before building the actual registration and login forms, you'll first specify how users are to be authenticated. With web applications for Internet users, you should use Forms authentication, instead of the Windows authentication that ASP.NET uses by default (see "Forms Versus Windows Authentication"). Changing the authentication mode of a web application from Windows to Forms requires changing the mode attribute of the authentication element in its *Web.config* file. You'll first need to add a *Web.config* file to your project.

To add a *Web.config* file to your project, right-click on the project in Solution Explorer and select Add New Item → Web Configuration File). Visual Studio will create and display the contents of the file.

Locate the <authentication> element in the file and change its mode attribute from Windows to Forms in the editor, as shown in Example 5-2.

Example 5-2. Setting Forms authentication

```
...
  <authentication mode="Forms"/>
  </system.web>
</configuration>
```

Forms Versus Windows Authentication

In Forms authentication, unauthenticated requests are redirected to a Web Form using HTTP client-side redirection. The user provides a username and password and then submits the form. If the application authenticates the request, the system issues a cookie containing the credentials or a key for reacquiring the identity. Subsequent requests are issued with the cookie in the request headers. They are then authenticated and authorized by an ASP. NET event handler using whatever validation method the application developer specifies.

In Windows authentication, ASP.NET works in conjunction with Microsoft Internet Information Services (IIS) authentication. Authentication is performed by IIS in one of three ways: basic, digest, or Integrated Windows Authentication. When IIS authentication is complete, ASP.NET uses the authenticated identity to authorize access.

It is not feasible for you to create separate Windows accounts for users using your application through the Internet. So Forms authentication is the preferred method for Internet applications.

4. To use the Profile service to store a user shopping cart, you need to define a profile property for the cart and specify its characteristics. To do that, add the markup shown in bold in Example 5-3 to *Web.config*.

Example 5-3. Defining the shoppingcart profile property

```
<system.web>
  <anonymousIdentification enabled="true"/>
    <profile>
      <properties>
        <add name="shoppingcart" allowAnonymous="true"
            type="OReilly.Cart" serializeAs="Xml"/>
      </properties>
    </profile>
    ...
```

You define the type for the shoppingcart profile property as OReilly. Cart. This type refers to the Cart class that you have defined in *ShoppingCart.vb*. The shoppingcart profile property will be serialized as an XML string so that it can be stored in a database.

 To save the value of an object to disk, you need to serialize it into XML or binary format. In this case, you've chosen the XML method.

The <anonymousIdentification> element must be added in addition to the shoppingcart property because an Internet user viewing your cart may not yet be an authenticated user of the application. To keep track of an unknown user, ASP.NET needs to assign a unique identifier to the anonymous user.

Attributes in the Profile Property

Besides defining the name and the type attributes for a profile property, which are both required (any .NET data type; default is string), you can also specify the following attributes:

readOnly
> Indicates whether the property is read-only.

serializeAs
> Represents how the property value should be stored in the database. Possible values are String (default), Xml, Binary, and ProviderSpecific.

provider
> Is the name of the profile provider to use.

defaultValue
> Is the default value of the property.

allowAnonymous
> Indicates whether the property can store values by anonymous users.

---

5. Switch to the code behind of *Main.aspx* and add the code for the imgBtn_Click method shown in Example 5-4. This method retrieves the shopping cart of the current user—whether authenticated or anonymous—and then adds the selected item to it. The updated shopping cart is then saved to the Profile object.

Example 5-4. Add to Cart button (imgBtn) Click event handler

```
Protected Sub imgBtn_Click( _
   ByVal sender As Object, _
   ByVal e As System.Web.UI.ImageClickEventArgs) _
   Handles imgBtn1.Click, imgBtn2.Click, imgBtn3.Click

      Dim myCart As OReilly.Cart
      '---retrieve the existing cart
      myCart = Profile.shoppingcart
      If myCart Is Nothing Then
          myCart = New OReilly.Cart
      End If

      Dim isbn As String
      Select Case CType(sender, ImageButton).ID
          Case "imgBtn1" : isbn = "0-596-00812-0"
          Case "imgBtn2" : isbn = "0-596-00757-4"
          Case "imgBtn3" : isbn = "0-596-10071-X"
      End Select
      lblMessage.Text = "You have added " & isbn

      myCart.AddItem(isbn, 1)
      '---save the cart back into the profile
      Profile.shoppingcart = myCart

End Sub
```

For simplicity, you will add an item selected by the user into the shopping cart, even though the item might already be present in the cart.

Note that this subroutine handles the click event of three ImageButton controls. This is accomplished by the Handles statement:

```
Handles imgBtn1.Click, imgBtn2.Click, imgBtn3.Click
```

When any of the ImageButton controls is clicked, this subroutine will check which control fired the event by first converting the sender object into an ImageButton control and then examining the ID (control name) of the control:

```
Select Case CType(sender, ImageButton).ID
    Case "imgBtn1" : isbn = "0-596-00812-0"
    Case "imgBtn2" : isbn = "0-596-00757-4"
    Case "imgBtn3" : isbn = "0-596-10071-X"
End Select
```

Of course, if you have a lot of titles on a page you can check the ISBN using a database, but for this simple example you will hardcode the information.

6. Code the Page_Load event so that when the page (*Main.aspx*) is loaded, it can check the Membership class to check to see if the user is authenticated and print out the related information about the user (see Example 5-5).

Example 5-5. ShoppingCart Page_Load event handler

```
Protected Sub Page_Load(ByVal sender As Object, ByVal e As System.EventArgs)
Handles Me.Load
    Dim user As MembershipUser = Membership.GetUser
    If user Is Nothing Then
        lblMessage.Text = "You have not logged in yet."
    Else
        lblMessage.Text = "Hello " & user.UserName
    End If
End Sub
```

If the user is authenticated, the GetUser method from the Membership class will return information about the authenticated user, or else it will return Nothing.

> The Membership class in ASP.NET 2.0 takes on the role of validating user credentials and managing user settings.

7. To test the application, select *Main.aspx* in Solution Explorer and then press F5. Since you haven't logged in yet, you should see the message "You have not logged in yet," as shown in Figure 5-16.

> If you wish to debug your web application (by using F5), you need to add a *Web.config* file to your project. By default, if there is no *Web.config* file when you try to debug your application, Visual Studio will prompt you to add one.

8. Add a few items into the shopping cart by clicking on the Add to Cart buttons, and the items will then be added to the Profile object. Refresh the *App_Data* folder in Solution Explorer and you will see the *ASPNETDB.MDF* database file (see Figure 5-17).

> Bear in mind that at this moment, you have not yet been authenticated and are therefore an *anonymous* user.

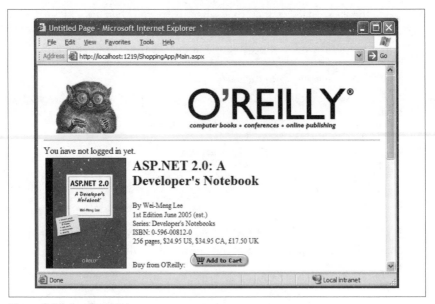

Figure 5-16. Loading Main.aspx

Figure 5-17. The ASPNETDB.MDF database file

9. Let's take a quick look at the information saved by the Profile object. Double-click on the *ASPNETDB.MDF* file. The Database Explorer window will appear, as shown in Figure 5-18. Expand the Tables item and locate the *aspnet_Profile* table. This table will contain the items saved in your shopping cart. Right-click on *aspnet_Profile* and select "Show Table Data."

Improved Debugging Support in ASP.NET 2.0

ASP.NET 1.x required you to explicitly set a start page for your project so that a specific page is loaded when you press F5 to debug the application. In ASP. NET 2.0, you can still set a specific page as the start page if you want. However, in ASP.NET 2.0 the start page by default is the currently selected page (currently selected either because you're editing it or because you selected the page in Solution Explorer). This feature saves you the trouble of setting a start page when you just want to debug a page you're working on at the moment.

This option is configurable via the project Property Pages dialog. To invoke it, right-click on the project name, *ShoppingApp*, in Solution Explorer and then select Property Pages. Select the Start Options item shown in the figure.

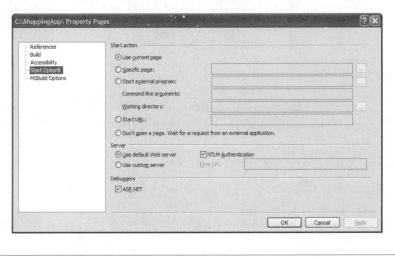

10. Notice that the shoppingcart profile property is saved as an XML string in the PropertyValuesString field (see Figure 5-19).

    The string itself is shown in Example 5-6.

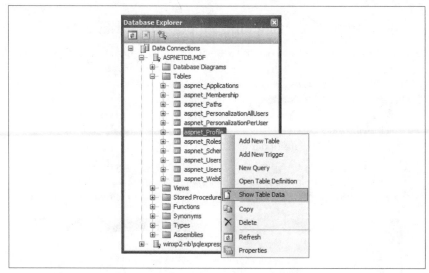

Figure 5-18. Viewing the content of the aspnet_Profile table

	UserId	PropertyNames	PropertyValuesS...	PropertyValuesBi...	LastUpdatedDate
	f341c8a2-af08-4bf3-b...	shoppingcart:S:0:493:	<?xml version="...	<Binary data>	4/21/2005 5:43:...

Figure 5-19. The content of the aspnet_Profile table

Example 5-6. Content of PropertyValuesString

```
<?xml version="1.0" encoding="utf-16"?>
<Cart xmlns:xsi="http://www.w3.org/2001/XMLSchema-instance" xmlns:xsd="http:
//www.w3.org/2001/XMLSchema">
  <items>
    <anyType xsi:type="itemType">
      <isbn>0-596-00812-0</isbn>
      <qty>1</qty>
    </anyType>
    <anyType xsi:type="itemType">
      <isbn>0-596-00757-4</isbn>
      <qty>1</qty>
    </anyType>
    <anyType xsi:type="itemType">
      <isbn>0-596-10071-X</isbn>
      <qty>1</qty>
    </anyType>
  </items>
</Cart>
```

11. The UserID of the user is a long string of characters (a GUID). You can verify this by looking into the *aspnet_Users* table (see Figure 5-20).

Figure 5-20. Content of the aspnet_Users table

Anonymous ID and GUID

If anonymous identification is enabled, when an un-authenticated user tries to save information into the Profile object, an anonymous user ID is generated for the user. This ID is a GUID (Globally Unique Identifier) that is guaranteed to be unique for each user.

You can programmatically retrieve the anonymous ID for the user via Request.AnonymousId.

Members Area

Now that anonymous users can visit your site and add items to the shopping cart, they need the ability to log in when they're ready to check out and purchase their selections. In this section you will create a checkout page that only authenticated users can access.

Creating New User Accounts

When a user has finished shopping (i.e., selecting items in the storefront), you need to some way to authenticate her so that you can retrieve particulars such as shipping address, credit card number, and so on. In this section, you will build a page through which the user can register as a member of your site.

1. First, as always, you need to create the registration page. Add a new Web Form to the project and name it *Register.aspx*. Select *MasterPage. master* as the Master Page once again to assure *Register.aspx* has the same look and feel as other pages on your site.

2. Drag and drop the CreateUserWizard control from the Login tab in the Toolbox onto the Content control in *Register.aspx*. The CreateUserWizard control is a visual control that prompts the user to supply the necessary information to create a new user account.

The CreateUserWizard control

Because creating user accounts is such as common task, one performed by most web sites, Microsoft has provided a new CreateUserWizard control in ASP.NET 2.0. The CreateUserWizard control takes the drudgery out of creating user accounts by providing a highly customizable control that accepts users' information. It performs such tasks as verifying users' passwords and authenticating email addresses. It then automatically adds user accounts to the site using the specified Membership Provider.

3. Now set the look and feel of the registration form. On the CreateUserWizard Tasks menu, click on the Auto Format... link to apply the Professional scheme to the control.

 ASP.NET 2.0 comes with several standard schemes to make your controls look professional.

4. You'll want the *Main.aspx* page to be loaded when the user has finished registering a new account. Set the ContinueDestinationPageUrl property (through the Properties window) of the CreateUserWizard control to *Main.aspx*.

5. Now position the control on the page. Highlight the CreateUserWizard control and select Format → Justify → Center on the Visual Studio menu bar to centralize the position of the control on the page. The *Register. aspx* page should now look like Figure 5-21.

Creating a Login Page

Once you have created a registration page, you'll want to create a login page so returning customers can log into the web site.

1. First, create the login page. Add a new Web Form to the project and name it *Login.aspx*. Select *MasterPage.master* as the Master Page once again to assure *Login.aspx* has the same look and feel as other pages on your site.

2. Now create a login form for users to complete. Drag and drop the Login control from the Login tab in the Toolbox onto the *Login.aspx* page. The Login control allows a user to log into your web site using the Membership class that you have seen earlier.

Figure 5-21. The Register.aspx page

New Login Controls in ASP.NET 2.0

ASP.NET 2.0 ships with several new Login controls (such as Login, LoginView, LoginStatus, LoginName, CreateUserWizard, and ChangePassword) to help you accomplish tasks such as user authentication, display of login status and login name, and more. The figure shows the various new Login controls in the Toolbox.

3. Set the look and feel of the control. Using the Login Tasks menu, click on the Auto Format... link to apply the Elegant scheme to the control.

4. Under the Login control, type the text "New Member? Register here." At the end of the text, add a LinkButton control from the Toolbox (see Figure 5-22).

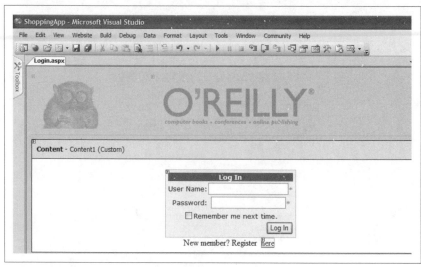

Figure 5-22. Populating the Login.aspx page

5. Finally, set the PostBackUrl property of the LinkButton control to *~/Register.aspx* so that the *Register.aspx* page will be loaded to help an unregistered user create a new account. Also, set the ContinueDestinationPageUrl property of the Login control to *Main.aspx* so that upon successful login, the user would be redirected to *Main.aspx*.

Restrict Unauthorized Access to Pages

So far, you have seen how to easily add a login page to your web site and how you can allow users to register for a new account in your application. In this section, you will add a new members-only folder to your web site and restrict access to authenticated users only.

1. First, create the folder in your project that will contain the restricted pages. To add a new folder to your project right-click on the project name, *ShoppingApp* in the Solution Explorer and then select Add Folder → Regular Folder. Name the folder *Members*.

2. Next, set the authorization required to access the folder. In *Web.config*, add the markup shown in bold in Example 5-7 to restrict anonymous users from accessing the files contained within the *Members* folder.

Example 5-7. Denying anonymous users access to the Members page

```
...
   </system.web>
   <location path="Members">
      <system.web>
         <authorization>
            <deny users="?" />
         </authorization>
      </system.web>
   </location>
</configuration>
```

The <location> element together with the <authorization> element allows you to restrict access to a particular folder on your web site. In this case, you have used the <deny> element to prevent all anonymous (represented by "?") users from accessing the *Members* folder.

Checking Out from the Store

While an unauthenticated user is selecting items on the Storefront page (*Main.aspx*) of *ShoppingApp* and adding them to the shopping cart, the Profile service treats the user as anonymous. Once the user has finished choosing items, clicks on the Checkout button to check out, and is authenticated, you need to take special steps to preserve the items he has added to the shopping cart. This is because the profile data that was saved while the user was anonymous is lost when he switches from using a GUID to using a user ID for identification. To migrate the profile of the user, you need to transfer whatever information was saved in the anonymous profile to the user profile.

In this section, you will learn how to migrate an anonymous profile to an authenticated profile once a user has been authenticated. Using the authenticated profile, you'll display a Checkout page that shows the user what's in the shopping cart and offers the option to continue shopping. The completed page is shown in Figure 5-25.

1. First, add a *Global.asax* file to the project (Figure 5-23). (Right-click on project name in Solution Explorer and then select Add New Item.... Select Global Application Class.) You will need the *Global.asax* file to service an event (see the next step) when the user changes from an anonymous state to an authenticated one. Visual Studio opens the file for you after adding it to your project.

Global.asax

The *Global.asax* file, also known as the ASP.NET application file, is an optional file that contains code for responding to application-level events raised by ASP.NET or by HttpModules. In this example, the Profile_ MigrateAnonymous event will be fired when a user changes from an anonymous state to an authenticated one. This event is serviced in the *Global.asax* file.

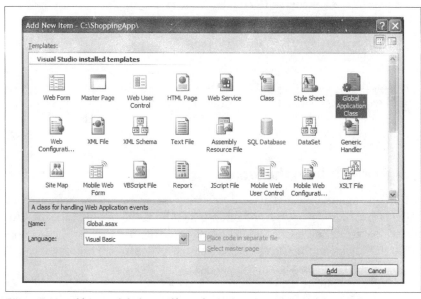

Figure 5-23. Adding a Global.asax file to the project

2. Type the Profile_MigrateAnonymous event handler shown in Example 5-8 into *Global.asax*. The Profile_MigrateAnonymous event is raised whenever a user changes her status from anonymous to authenticated (when she logs into the application via the *Login.aspx* page).

You can get the anonymous ID from the AnonymousId property (in the ProfileMigrateEventArgs class) and then use the GetProfile method to retrieve the anonymous profile. The retrieved profile can then be assigned to the authenticated user profile. You will also delete the old profile associated with the anonymous user.

Example 5-8. Profile_MigrateAnonymous event handler

```
Sub Profile_MigrateAnonymous(ByVal sender As Object, _
    ByVal e As ProfileMigrateEventArgs)
        Dim anonymousProfile As ProfileCommon = _
```

Example 5-8. Profile_MigrateAnonymous event handler (continued)

```
        Profile.GetProfile(e.AnonymousID)

    If anonymousProfile.shoppingcart IsNot Nothing Then
        Profile.shoppingcart = anonymousProfile.shoppingcart
    End If

    '---delete the items associated with the anonymous user
    ProfileManager.DeleteProfile(e.AnonymousID)

    '---clear the anonymous identifier from the request
    '    so that this event will not fire for an authenticated
    '    user
    AnonymousIdentificationModule.ClearAnonymousIdentifier
End Sub
```

3. Now you'll create the Checkout page that will be used to display the items currently stored in the user's shopping cart. Add a new Web Form to the *Members* folder and select the *MasterPage.master* Master Page. Name the new Web Form *Checkout.aspx*.

    Populate the form with a GridView control and apply the Sand & Sky scheme to it. (Select Auto Format... in the GridView Tasks menu; see Figure 5-24.)

Figure 5-24. Applying Auto Format to a GridView control

Also, add a LinkButton control under the GridView control and set its Text property to "Continue Shopping" and its PostBackUrl property to *~/Main.aspx*. The results are shown in Figure 5-25.

> The GridView control in ASP.NET 2.0 is similar to the DataGridView control you have seen in Chapter 4, except that GridView is web based and DataGridView is Windows based.

4. In the code behind of *Checkout.aspx*, code the Form_Load event as shown in Example 5-9. The *Checkout.aspx* page will first create a dataset containing all the items in the shopping cart and then use it to bind to the GridView control. It also changes the image in the imgHeader control in the Master Page using the FindControl method in the Master property.

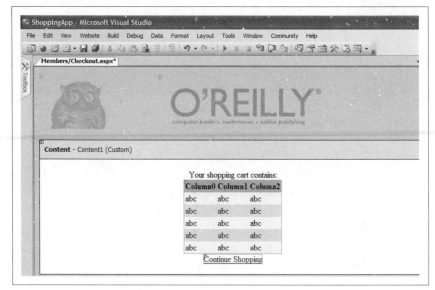

Figure 5-25. Members/Checkout.aspx page

Example 5-9. Checkout.aspx Form_Load event

```
Imports System.Data

Protected Sub Page_Load(ByVal sender As Object, _
   ByVal e As System.EventArgs) Handles Me.Load
      Dim myCart As OReilly.Cart
      myCart = Profile.shoppingcart
      Dim item As OReilly.itemType

      '---change the image
      Dim masterImage As Image
      masterImage = CType(Master.FindControl("imgHeader"), _
                  Image)
      If masterImage IsNot Nothing Then
          masterImage.ImageUrl = "~/Images/header_shopping.gif"
      End If

      '---create a dataset---
      Dim ds As New DataSet
      ds.Tables.Add("Items")
      ds.Tables("Items").Columns.Add("ISBN")
      ds.Tables("Items").Columns.Add("Qty")
      Dim row As DataRow

      '---return all the items as a dataset---
      For Each item In myCart.items
          row = ds.Tables("Items").NewRow
          row("ISBN") = item.isbn
```

Example 5-9. Checkout.aspx Form_Load event (continued)

```
        row("Qty") = item.qty
        ds.Tables("Items").Rows.Add(row)
    Next

    '---Bind the GridView control to the dataset
    GridView1.DataSource = ds
    GridView1.DataBind( )

End Sub
```

 Think of a dataset as a database containing tables stored in memory.

Modifying a Master Page at Runtime

When a Web Form that uses a Master Page is loaded at runtime, it displays the content of the Master Page together with its own content. However there are times when you will want to modify parts of the Master Page when a particular Content page is loaded.

You locate the controls you want to modify on the Master Page by using the FindControl method of the Master property, then supplying the name and type of the control you want to modify. Once the control is located, you can change its properties as if it were a local object.

Master is a special property exposed by the Web Form as a handle with which to access the Master Page. However, the Master property is valid only on pages that reference a Master Page.

You can programmatically check if a page is using a Master Page by doing this:

```
    If Master Is Nothing Then
        '---Page does not use master page---
        ...
    End If
```

---

5. You'll want *Checkout.aspx* to be displayed when a user clicks on the Checkout button in *Main.aspx*. So, as a last step, go to *Main.aspx* and set the PostPackUrl property of the Checkout button in *Main.aspx* to ~/ *Members/Checkout.aspx* so that the user can be brought to the *Checkout.aspx* page to check out. If an unauthenticated user clicks on the Checkout button, he will be redirected to *Login.aspx*.

Testing the Application

With the entire application built, it is now time to test it out.

1. To get started, select *Main.aspx* in Solution Explorer and then press F5 to debug the application.

2. In *Main.aspx*, add a few items into the shopping cart, as shown in Figure 5-26.

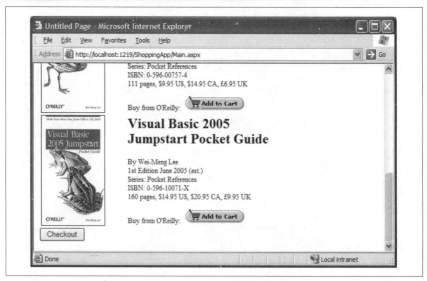

Figure 5-26. Adding items to a shopping cart and then checking out

3. When you are done adding the items, click the Checkout button and you will be redirected to the *Login.aspx* page (see Figure 5-27).

4. Since you have not registered for an account yet, click on the "here" link to load the *Register.aspx* page (see Figure 5-28). Enter the required information and click Create User.

You should use a strong password consisting of a mixture of alphanumeric values and special characters. For example, you can use password such as pass@word1. ASP.NET 2.0 requires passwords to have a mixture of numerals (0–9), letters (a–z, A–Z), and special characters (such as # and !). It will also reject passwords that are less than seven characters.

Default Login Page

Wait a minute, how does ASP.NET know that it should load the *Login.aspx* page to authenticate the user when the Checkout button is clicked, rather than the other pages?

Well, in ASP.NET 2.0, a page with the filename *Login.aspx* is deemed to be the login page when users try to access restricted folders (*Members*, in this case). This special name *Login.aspx* (plus many others) is "burned" into ASP. NET as a default.

The *machine.config.default* file (located in *C:\WINDOWS\Microsoft.NET\ Framework\<version>\CONFIG*) contains all the default system-wide configuration settings. To see the default settings defined in *machine.config.default*, check the *machine.config.comments* file (also in the same directory) for details.

For example, the default settings for Forms authentication found in *machine. config.comments* are:

```
<forms
    name=".ASPXAUTH"
    loginUrl="login.aspx"
    protection="All"
    timeout="30"
    path="/"
    requireSSL="false"
    slidingExpiration="true"
    defaultUrl="default.aspx"
    cookieless="UseCookies"
    enableCrossAppRedirects="false" >
```

If you want to override the default settings, you should modify *machine.config* (for machine-wide configuration) or *Web.config* (for application-wide configuration). The rationale for splitting the original *machine.config* file into three different files is to reduce the size of *machine.config* and hence improve performance.

5. If the registration is successful, you will see the page shown in Figure 5-29. Click Continue to return to the *Main.aspx* page.

6. In *Main.aspx*, if you now click on the Checkout button, you will be redirected to the *Checkout.aspx* page (see Figure 5-30). All the items that you have added before you log in are now displayed in the GridView control. You can click on the Continue Shopping link to return to *Main. aspx* to continue adding items into your shopping cart.

Figure 5-27. The Login.aspx page

Figure 5-28. The Register.aspx page

Figure 5-29. Registration successful

Figure 5-30. The Checkout.aspx page

Summary

In this chapter, you built a simple e-commerce application that uses some of the new features in ASP.NET 2.0. You have seen how to use a Master Page to maintain a consistent look and feel for the pages in your site. You have also seen how information about users can be persisted using the Profile service. Last but not least, you have learned how easy it is to implement security in your web applications using the new set of security controls built to work with the underlying Membership class.

CHAPTER 6

Moving from VB 6 to VB 2005

To take the plunge and move your current VB 6 application to VB 2005 requires more than just a cursory overview of the capabilities of the language. Each type of application currently deployed in your environment warrants different considerations. In this chapter, I will discuss some of the factors you need to consider before upgrading your current application to VB 2005. I will also discuss various upgrade strategies that you can take should you decide to use VB 2005. This chapter will end with a look at using the Code Advisor for Visual Basic 6.0 and the Visual Basic Upgrade Wizard to upgrade your VB 6 application to VB 2005.

Migrate, Replace, Rewrite, or Reuse?

Once an organization has decided that a certain application no longer meets its business needs and that doing nothing is no longer an option, modernization comes into play.* There are at least four ways to approach the modernization of a VB application that should be considered. The deciding factors are:

- The quality of the application code
- The business value of the application

Quality in this case is about the suitability of the application in business and technical terms and should be assessed in accordance with the following parameters:

Current effectiveness of application
Generated errors, number of workarounds, and level of support needed.

---

* The following section is an excerpt from the "Designing an Application Migration Strategy for Visual Basic 6.0 to Visual Basic .NET" whitepaper authored by ArtinSoft, published on MSDN at *http:// msdn.microsoft.com/library/default.asp?url=/library/en-us/dv_vstechart/html/appmigrationstrat.asp.*

Stability and completeness of core business rules

Will the application logic remain the same in the foreseeable future? An underlying assumption in this paper is that the current software asset is a valuable one. If the business model is going to change substantially, then this assumption has to be called into question. In practice, the code is often the only repository of business rules and these are scattered throughout the code. Thus any attempt to "start from scratch" needs to reconstruct and document the requirements captured in the current code and take these requirements as the starting point for the negotiation of new requirements.

Stage of the lifecycle

In the earlier stages of its lifecycle, an application will likely map closely to its functionality requirements, although the platform could be obsolete.

Development environment

The development team and the environmental capabilities required to successfully deliver a modernization project need to be assessed. Here, the developer's knowledge regarding the application source code, the target technologies, and the resolution of modernization issues identified during the code assessment are crucial. In general, it is recommended that developers executing the project be fully trained in VB 2005. Additionally, other factors such as the existence of test cases must be considered.

The business value of the application is another important consideration and this will depend to a considerable degree on its uniqueness. If the quality of the application is poor and there is comparable functionality available in a third-party software package, it makes sense to replace it.

There are four broad modernization options—*migrate, re-use, rewrite,* or *replace*—any one of which can be the right choice either for a complete application or for parts of an application. Figure 6-1 shows how the decision factors correlate with the modernization path.

Migrate

If the VB application meets current business needs and its quality is good, chances are the application can be effectively modernized to continue to meet the needs of the business in the future. In such cases, a migration process can be applied and then functionality and business reach can be added as needed. In this chapter, when we refer to a migration or an upgrade, we are referring to an automatically assisted migration using the Microsoft Visual Basic Upgrade Wizard that is integrated in Visual Studio .NET (see "Upgrading VB 6 Applications," later in this chapter).

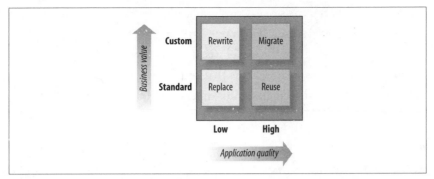

Figure 6-1. Modernization options chart

Reuse

There are two possibilities here, one in which the application is centered on a third-party package/DBMS already, and the other in which the business has developed its own application from scratch. If the VB 6 application portfolio is largely centered on a third-party package, then the best way to move forward may be to upgrade to the latest version and use wrapping techniques to provide the required reach and other functionality improvements. For in-house applications, consider wrapping the application pieces and integrating them with new development.

Rewrite

The key asset here is the business rules and data structures; the application is the problem. Application mining and analysis of code logic and data structures is required to provide the starting point for the rewrite.

Replace

Look for a suitable package or outsource. Be prepared to make changes to the business model to meet the package half way.

Making the Right Decision

Upon the initiation of the project you should prepare a feasibility analysis that provides an assessment of the business and technical quality of the application. The following series of checklists presents some of the questions that you should consider when choosing one of the alternatives.

Migrate

Below is the checklist for choosing to migrate:

❏ Existing application fulfills current business needs

❏ Moderate functionality changes needed in existing application

- ❏ High operational costs of existing application
- ❏ Need to migrate to the .NET Framework for strategic reasons
- ❏ Future vision includes the use of web services or web access
- ❏ Stable code base and a test suite that certifies it
- ❏ Resources needed to maintain or amend applications on existing platform are difficult to find

Reuse

Below is the checklist for choosing to reuse:

- ❏ Business rules satisfactory
- ❏ Low operational costs of existing application
- ❏ Simple web access required, allowing a wrapping solution
- ❏ Have resources to keep core Visual Basic 6.0 application maintained
- ❏ Off-the-shelf software central to existing, rely on a third party to support and maintain

Rewrite

Below is the checklist for choosing to rewrite:

- ❏ Functionality does not meet business needs
- ❏ No off-the-shelf solution comes close to meeting needs
- ❏ Poor quality code in existing platform and high maintenance costs
- ❏ Can afford time, cost, and disruption involved
- ❏ Need to use the Microsoft .NET Framework for strategic reasons
- ❏ Future vision includes the use of web services

Replace

Below is the checklist for choosing to replace:

- ❏ Application significantly out of line with business needs
- ❏ Willing to make changes to business model to fit off-the-shelf solution or availability of off-the-shelf solution that closely fit your business requirements
- ❏ Can afford time, cost, and disruption involved

The preceding questions can apply to complete applications or to discrete parts of applications. Typically a large application will require use of more than one modernization alternative. When deciding the best path for a particular part of an application, bear in mind that many developers will invariably say that rewriting your application is the best solution if you need to upgrade it, because they usually feel they can write it better the second time, armed with the benefit of hindsight. Certainly if the application is poorly designed, rewriting it can be a good option because it provides an opportunity to do it right. However, examining the business case for upgrading, rewriting, replacing, or leaving the application in Visual Basic 6.0 always provides some interesting insights.

If the application already supports your business needs, doesn't require enhancements to its functionality, and if you already have support staff trained in VB 6, then leaving the application in VB 6 is a good option. Nevertheless, your organization needs to assess the risks of this approach in light of current lifecycle guidelines from Microsoft and the opportunities that the VB 2005 and .NET framework offer to your organization.

If there is a business need to move the application to VB 2005, then there is a need to look more closely at rewriting versus upgrading. Upgrading the application using the VB 6 to VB 2005 migration tool is a cost-effective way to migrate your applications. One popular reason for moving an application to VB 2005 is to either web-enable the application, or to enhance an existing web-enabled application with ASP.NET features such as tracing, flexible state management, scaleable data access, and improved performance. As mentioned previously, rewriting sometimes yields an improved application. The downside is that the development cost will be much greater than upgrading.

There are some benefits to rewriting. Rewriting allows you to correct a poor design, and COM objects can be replaced with .NET objects that are more scaleable and don't require registration during deployment. The flipside of this is that upgrading is much quicker and COM objects can be replaced with .NET objects after the upgrade has taken place.

In brief, you have to decide on how to move forward with your modernization project. If you decide that the best solution is to leave the application in VB 6, then you are done! On the other hand, if you have assessed that the best solution is to rewrite your application, then the best piece of advice is to make sure that you follow an accepted development methodology and that you really look back at the issue your current application has to make sure you can leverage that knowledge when moving forward. If you think your current application and its source code have value, and that by moving it to .NET you can extend its lifecycle, then you have decided that automatically assisted migration is the best solution for your code. Finally, you may decide to go for a combination of the above solutions, as is the case for most modernization projects.

Using COM Objects in VB 2005

One of the primary reasons VB 6 programmers and their companies are reluctant to migrate to VB 2005 is the huge investments they have made in developing COM components. However, COM components continue to be supported in .NET. In the following sections, you will see how you can use legacy COM components in your VB 2005 applications.

The most direct way to use COM objects in VB 2005 is to use *COM Interop*. Although applications that run under the .NET Framework can only work with .NET components, .NET allows you to use your existing COM components by means of a *Runtime Callable Wrapper* (RCW). When you use RCW to interact with a COM object, an assembly is used as a wrapper for the COM object. The RCW acts as a bridge between the unmanaged code (the COM object) and managed code (your .NET application), and all communications with the COM object are routed through this class (see Figure 6-2).

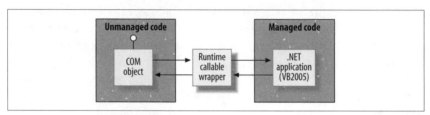

Figure 6-2. Runtime Callable Wrapper

 COM objects are unmanaged code, therefore you need to remember to free up their resources when they are no longer in use.

To illustrate the support of COM in .NET, let's consider a simple example.

Suppose you want to display a PDF file in a VB 2005 Windows application. To do so, you can make use of the Adobe Acrobat Browser Document control (which is a COM object) installed on your system (the component is installed on your computer when you install the Adobe Acrobat Reader).

First, create a new Windows application. To use the Adobe COM component, look for it and select it from the list of COM components on your system. To see the list, click the COM tag of the Add Reference dialog in Solution Explorer in Visual Studio 2005, as shown in Figure 6-3. Click OK.

Drag and drop the Adobe Acrobat 7.0 Browser Document, which is now located in the Toolbox under the All Windows Forms tab, onto your Windows Form (Form1, unless you have renamed it). The result is shown in Figure 6-4.

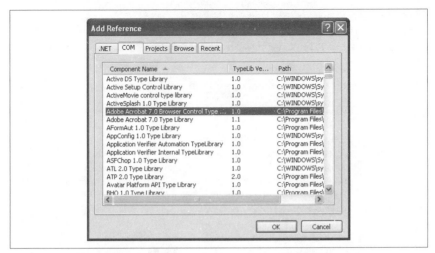

Figure 6-3. Add a COM component to your project

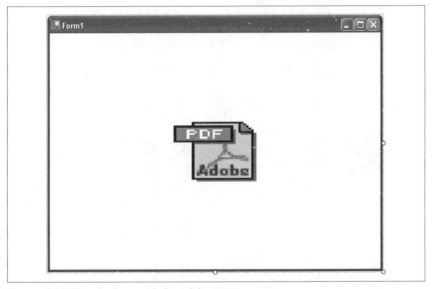

Figure 6-4. Filling the form with the Adobe COM component

To display a PDF document using the control, double-click on the Windows Form and code the Load event as shown in Example 6-1.

Example 6-1. Form1 Load event handler

```
Private Sub Form1_Load( _
    ByVal sender As System.Object, _
    ByVal e As System.EventArgs) _
    Handles MyBase.Load, _
```

Example 6-1. Form1 Load event handler (continued)

```
    MyBase.Load
        AxAcroPDF1.LoadFile("C:\MiniReader.pdf")
End Sub
```

There isn't much difference in coding; your COM component is used much like a .NET component.

 Besides exposing using COM components in a .NET application, you can also use .NET Components in a COM application via the COM Callable Wrapper (CCW). The CCW is used to marshal calls between managed and unmanaged code (see Figure 6-5), thereby allowing COM applications to make use of .NET components.

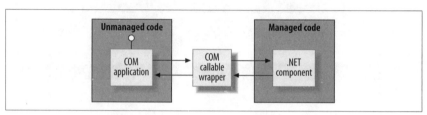

Figure 6-5. COM Callable Wrapper

Figure 6-6 shows what happens when the application is run.

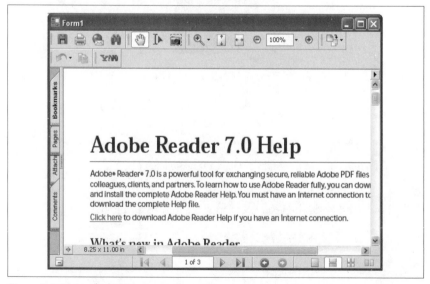

Figure 6-6. Using the COM component

Not only does COM interop make it easy to use COM components in your VB 2005 application, it also does away with the error-prone task of installing and registering COM components on target computers through a new feature known as *RegFree COM* (Registration-Free COM).

 RegFree COM runs only on Windows XP and later releases of the Windows operating system.

Using RegFree COM, you can deploy an application that uses a COM component without registering it on the user's machine, thus avoiding the notorius collection of problems commonly referred to as "DLL Hell." *RegFree COM* even allows you to run multiple versions of a COM component on the same machine.

 RegFree COM works by automatically generating a manifest from the COM component's type library and component registration on the developer's machine. Therefore, while it is not required to install the component on the end users' machines, a copy must be registered on the developer's machine.

To enable use of RegFree COM, all COM components referenced in Visual Studio 2005 now have a new Isolated property (see Figure 6-7). If you set Isolated to true, the component can be deployed through ClickOnce, and Visual Studio 2005 will automatically do all the work to deploy the COM component onto the target machine (without needing to register it on the target machine).

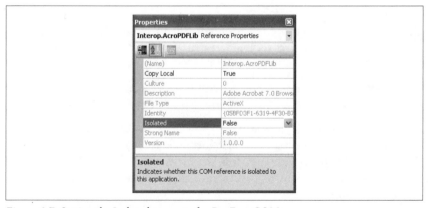

Figure 6-7. Setting the Isolated property for RegFree COM

Upgrading VB 6 Applications

To make it easier for you to upgrade your VB 6 applications, Microsoft provides made two free tools:

Code Advisor for Visual Basic 6.0
> An add-on for Visual Studio 6.0 that reviews your existing VB 6 code to ensure it meets predetermined coding standards.

Upgrade Wizard
> A built-in Visual Studio 2005 tool that automatically upgrades your VB 6 applications when you open them in Visual Studio 2005. The Upgrade Wizard will upgrade your VB 6 code to VB 2005 and flag those code blocks that need further attention.

Before you upgrade your VB 6 application, you should first run your application through the Code Advisor for VB 6 and fix any ambiguous code it identifies that will possibly make the upgrade process difficult. Then, open your VB 6 application in Visual Studio 2005 so that the Upgrade Wizard can upgrade your code to VB 2005.

Using Code Advisor for VB 6

The first step toward upgrading your VB 6 applications to VB 2005 is to run the Code Advisor for Visual Basic 6.0. The Code Advisor for Visual Basic 6 is an add-on for Visual Studio 6.0 that is used to review your code to ensure that it meets predetermined coding standards. The coding standards are based on best practices developed by Microsoft to produce robust and easy-to-maintain code. You can download this free tool from: *http://www. microsoft.com/downloads/details.aspx?FamilyID=a656371a-b5c0-4d40-b015-0caa02634fae&DisplayLang=en*.

Once the Code Advisor for VB 6 is downloaded and installed, you will find a new set of buttons in the toolbar area of Visual Studio 6.0, as shown in Figure 6-8.

The Scope Definition button allows you to use Code Advisor to check the entire project, or to check only the currently active file.

To see how the Code Advisor for VB 6 works, consider the following simple VB 6 application consisting of a single form (Hello Application) as shown in Figure 6-9. The form contains four controls, including a Label control (lblMessage), a Text control (txtName), a Hello button (cmdHello), and an Exit button (cmdExit).

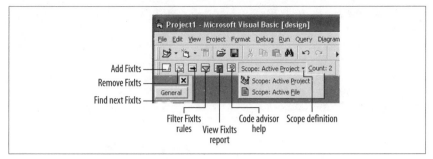

Figure 6-8. The Code Advisor toolbar

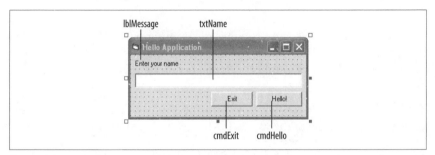

Figure 6-9. An application in VB 6

When the Exit button is clicked, the form displays a message box that asks users if they want to exit, as shown in Example 6-2.

Example 6-2. Exit button Click event handler

```
Private Sub cmdExit_Click( )
    response = MsgBox("Exit program?", vbYesNo)
    If response = vbYes Then
        End
    End If
End Sub
```

This VB 6 application also uses a subroutine to display a message via the MsgBox function, as shown in Example 6-3. Note that this function uses the default ByRef to pass in parameters by reference.

Example 6-3. DisplayMsg subroutine

```
Public Sub DisplayMsg(str As String)
    MsgBox str
End Sub
```

When the Hello button is clicked, the TextBox control is assigned to an object of type Object. A comparison is then performed to check if the Text property (not explicitly specified as it is the default property) in the TextBox control is empty. The relevant message is then printed. The code is shown in Example 6-4.

Example 6-4. Hello button Click event handler

```
Private Sub cmdHello_Click( )
    Dim obj As Object
    Set obj = txtName
    If obj = "" Then
        DisplayMsg ("Please enter your name")
    Else
        DisplayMsg ("Hello " & txtName)
    End If
End Sub
```

To use the Code Advisor to examine the application, click the Add FixIts button. The toolbar will display the number of issues (known as FixIts) that Code Advisor has raised (in this example, two FixIts were raised—Count:2), as shown in Figure 6-8.

To examine the FixIts raised, switch to the Code view where you will see comments prefixed with the word "FIXIT" as shown in Example 6-5.

Example 6-5. Hello and Exit button Click event handler FIXITs

```
'FIXIT: Use Option Explicit to avoid implicitly
' creating variables of type Variant
' FixIT90210ae-R383-H1984

Private Sub cmdExit_Click( )
    response = MsgBox("Exit program?", vbYesNo)
    If response = vbYes Then
        End
    End If
End Sub

Public Sub DisplayMsg(str As String)
    MsgBox str
End Sub

Private Sub cmdHello_Click( )
'FIXIT: Declare 'obj' with an early-bound data type
'FixIT90210ae-R1672-R1B8ZE
    Dim obj As Object
    Set obj = txtName
    If obj = "" Then
        DisplayMsg ("Please enter your name")
    Else
        DisplayMsg ("Hello " & txtName)
    End If
End Sub
```

Using the Code Advisor toolbar, you can remove all FixIts by clicking the Remove FixIts button, or find the next FixIts by clicking the Find Next Fix-Its button.

In this example, the two specific FixIts are:

- You should use Option Explicit to prevent your code from using undeclared variables. Once this is done, the response variable should be explicitly declared.

- The obj variable should be declared as a TextBox for early binding.

To view a summary of the FixIts raised, you can click on the View FixIt Report button. The report is shown as a web page (see Figure 6-10).

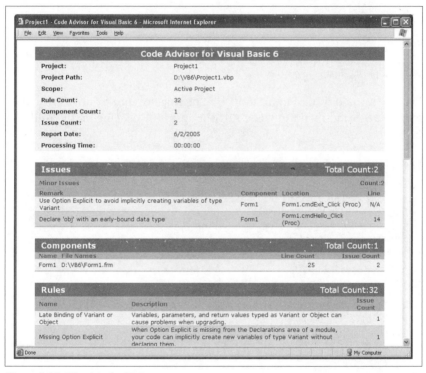

Figure 6-10. Viewing the FixIts report

You can customize the Code Advisor (click on Filter FixIts Rules) to examine your code using a specific version of Visual Basic (Visual Basic .NET 2002 or Visual Basic.NET 2003), or based on best practices (see Figure 6-11).

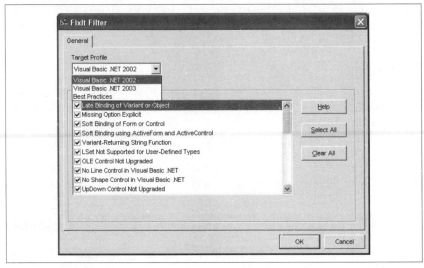

Figure 6-11. Customizing Code Advisor

Let's now modify the application by entering to code shown in bold in Example 6-6 and then run Code Advisor again (by clicking on the Add Fix-Its button).

Example 6-6. Modified Hello and Exit button Click event handlers

```
Option Explicit
Private Sub cmdExit_Click()
    Dim response As VbMsgBoxResult
    response = MsgBox("Exit program?", vbYesNo)
    If response = vbYes Then
        End
    End If
End Sub

Public Sub DisplayMsg(str As String)
    MsgBox str
End Sub

Private Sub cmdHello_Click()
    Dim obj As TextBox
    Set obj = txtName
    If obj = "" Then
        DisplayMsg ("Please enter your name")
    Else
        DisplayMsg ("Hello " & txtName)
    End If
End Sub
```

This time, the application passes the Code Advisor's check. You can now proceed to the next step of the upgrading process: using the Upgrade Wizard to upgrade the code to VB 2005.

Using the Upgrade Wizard

When you try to open a Visual Basic project (Windows, web, or other) created with a previous version of Visual Studio (Visual Studio 6 or Visual Studio .NET), Visual Studio 2005 will launch the Upgrade Wizard and attempt to upgrade the project to VB 2005. The Upgrade Wizard will automatically upgrade your code to VB 2005, and anything else that is ambiguous will be marked with comments and displayed in the Upgrade Report.

To see how the Upgrade Wizard works, let's upgrade the application discussed in "Using Code Advisor for VB 6." You'll use Visual Studio 2005 to open this VB project. When it's opened in Visual Studio 2005, the Upgrade Wizard will kick into action, as shown in Figure 6-12.

Figure 6-12. The Visual Basic Upgrade Wizard

The Upgrade Wizard will lead you through a series of steps to upgrade the VB 6 project. When you have finished, your VB 6 project will be displayed in Visual Studio 2005.

Figure 6-13 shows the project after it has been upgraded to VB 2005.

Figure 6-13. The upgraded VB project

In Solution Explorer, note that a new item has been added to the project: _UpgradeReport.htm. The _UpgradeReport.htm document lists the changes made to the original project and highlights the various issues encountered during the upgrade process, as shown in Figure 6-14.

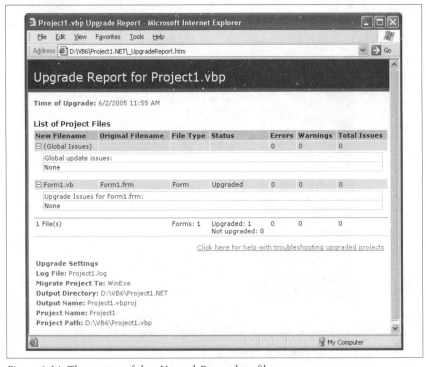

Figure 6-14. The content of the _UpgradeReport.htm file

Let's look at the upgraded code and observe some of the salient changes, as shown in Example 6-7. The comments and code added by the Upgrade Wizard are highlighted in bold.

Example 6-7. The upgraded project

```vbnet
Option Strict Off
Option Explicit On
Friend Class Form1
    Inherits System.Windows.Forms.Form

    Private Sub cmdExit_Click( _
        ByVal eventSender As System.Object, _
        ByVal eventArgs As System.EventArgs) _
        Handles cmdExit.Click
        Dim response As MsgBoxResult
        response = MsgBox("Exit program?", MsgBoxStyle.YesNo)
        If response = MsgBoxResult.Yes Then
            End
        End If
    End Sub

    'UPGRADE_NOTE: str was upgraded to str_Renamed.
    'Click for more: 'ms-help://MS.VSCC.v80/dv_commoner/local/
    'redirect.htm?keyword="A9E4979A-37FA-4718-9994-97DD76ED70A7"'
    Public Sub DisplayMsg(ByRef str_Renamed As String)
        MsgBox(str_Renamed)
    End Sub

    Private Sub cmdHello_Click( _
        ByVal eventSender As System.Object, _
        ByVal eventArgs As System.EventArgs) _
        Handles cmdHello.Click
        Dim obj As System.Windows.Forms.TextBox
        obj = txtName
        If obj.Text = "" Then
            DisplayMsg(("Please enter your name"))
        Else
            DisplayMsg(("Hello " & txtName.Text))
        End If
    End Sub
End Class
```

Note that while there is only one upgrade note in this project, several changes have been made to the code:

- The variable str in the DisplayMsg subroutine has been renamed and the ByRef keyword has been inserted. You should always explicitly specify the ByRef or ByVal keyword before you upgrade so that you don't get unexpected results.

- The Option Strict Off statement is inserted into the code. As the Option Strict statement is not supported in VB 6, it is turned off by default in VB 2005. Ideally, you should turn it on so that all narrowing conversions are flagged (see Chapter 2 for details).

- The constants vbYesNo and vbYes have been changed to MsgBoxStyle. YesNo and MsgBoxResult.Yes, respectively.

- The Text property has been explicitly added to the obj and txtName variables.

What you have seen here is a superficial view of the support the Visual Basic Upgrade Wizard can provide. For more details, check out this article at: *http://msdn.microsoft.com/library/default.asp?url=/library/en-us/dv_vstechart/ html/vstchexpvsnetlab5.asp.*

 Note that the Visual Basic Upgrade Wizard can only upgrade applications written in VB 6 and later. As such, if you want to upgrade applications written in a version of Visual Basic released prior to VB 6, you need to first upgrade them to VB 6 before using the Upgrade Wizard.

Summary

In this chapter, you have been introduced to several factors you need to consider before deciding whether or how to enhance your VB applications to meet future business needs. The various checklists provided here and others available from Microsoft will help you decide whether to migrate, replace, rewrite, or reuse an existing VB 6 application. You have also learned how you can continue to use COM objects—legacy or otherwise—in a VB 2005 application. Finally, you have seen how two tools provided by Microsoft (Code Advisor for VB 6 and Upgrade Wizard) can help you upgrade your applications from VB 6 to VB 2005, once you've decided to do so.

Index

Symbols

& (ampersand)
  concatenation operator, 41
  type character, 34
* (asterisk) multiplication operator, 41
@ (at sign) type character, 34
/ (backslash) division operator, 41
^ (caret) exponentiation operator, 41
: (colon), grouping statements using, 44
$ (dollar sign) type character, 34
= (equal sign) assignment
       operator/equality operator, 41
! (exclamation point) type character, 34
> greater-than operator, 41
>= greater-than-or-equal-to
       operator, 41
(hash mark)
  assigning dates/times, 35
  type character, 34
< less-than operator, 41
<= less-than-or-equal-to operator, 41
– (minus) subtraction operator, 41
&= operator, 41
*= operator, 41
+= operator, 41
-= operator, 41
/= operator, 41
\= operator, 41
^= operator, 41
% (percent) type character, 34
+ (plus) addition
       operator/concatenation
       operator, 41
" (quotation character), representing in
       string variables, 35
\ (slash) integer division operator, 41
_ (underscore) character, 38
< > not-equal-to operator, 41

A

About boxes, adding to
       applications, 21–24
abstract classes
  specifying implementation details
    with, 90–92
  vs. interfaces, 92
abstract methods, 91
AcceptButton property, 14
access modifiers, 85–87
Add Web Reference window, 111
AddressOf operator, 42
AddTitle method, 119
aggregating data types using
       structures, 87–88
All tab (IntelliSense), 18
allowAnonymous attribute (profile
       property), 151
Amazon Web Services Licenses
       Agreement, 117
Amazon.com
  accessing asynchronously, 130–134
  accessing web services of, 112–116
  adding web references to, 111
Anchor property, setting for various
       controls, 109–110

We'd like to hear your suggestions for improving our indexes. Send email to *index@oreilly.com*.

And operator, 42
AndAlso operator, 42, 45
anonymous profiles, migrating to
        authenticated
        profiles, 161–165
anonymous user IDs and GUID, 157
AnonymousId property
        (ProfileMigrateEventArgs
        class), 162
<anonymousIdentification>
        element, 151
app.config file, 26–27
Application Settings feature, 25
applications
    adding About boxes to, 21–24
    debugging, 18
    quitting, 13–15
    running, 18
    saving state of, 24–27
arguments
    optional, 51
    passing by reference, 50
    passing by value, 49
arithmetic operators, 41
arrays in VB 2005, 38
As keyword, 31
ASP.NET 2.0, building web applications
        with, 136–170
aspnet_Users table, 157
assemblies, 60
assignment operators, 41
attributes, tagging objects with, 95–97
audio files, playing, 54
authenticated users, restricting access
        to, 160
<authentication> element, 149
authentication, Forms vs.
        Windows, 150
AutoCorrect feature, 74
automatic data binding, 6–12
automatically updating
        applications, 130–135

B

BackgroundWorker control, 99,
        130–134
base classes, 67
binding data to forms, 105–110,
        122–124
BindingNavigator control, 10, 108, 122

blocking calls, 130
Boolean type, 30
BorderStyle property
        lblISBN control, 110
        SplitContainer control, 102
branching statements, 43–46
breakpoints, setting, 19
browsing records, 6–12
btnAddTitle control, 110
btnGetInfo control, 110, 113
btnViewCatalog control, 110
Button control, 123
ByRef keyword, 181, 187
Byte type, 30

C

Cancel button, linking events with, 17
Cancel_Button control, property of, 15
CancelButton property, 14
casting (type conversion), 39
catching errors with Try-Catch-Finally
        statements, 52
CCWs (COM Callable Wrappers), 178
ChangePassword control, 159
Char type, 30
Checked property (chkShowCover
        control), 110
child classes, 67
chkAutoAdd control, 110
chkShowCover control, 110
Class Designer, 82
classes, 59
    access modifiers and, 85–87
    adding properties to, 73–75
    controlling implementation
        of, 89–97
    customizing, 66–81
    defining, 82–85
    designing, 81–88
    generic classes, 77
    instantiating, 63
    .NET Framework Class
        Library, 60–62
    overloading methods, 69
    Partial classes, 78–81
    reusing, 67
    splitting up physical implementation
        of, 78–81
    vs. structures, 88
Class_Initialize method, 73

Class_Terminate method, 93
ClickOnce feature, 99, 125–127
Close buttons
 adding to forms, 123
 linking events with, 16
Close window buttons, confirmation
  when using, 13–15
CLR (Common Language Runtime), 60
Code Advisor for Visual Basic
  6.0, 180–185
code reuse
 generic classes and, 79
 inheritance, 67
Code view for web forms, 142
code-behind pages, 15
 My namespace, 28
COM Callable Wrappers (CCWs), 178
COM Interop, using in VB 2005, 176
COM objects, using in VB
  2005, 176–179
Common Language Runtime (CLR), 60
Common tab (IntelliSense), 18
comparison operators, 41
compile-time errors, 51
concatenation operators, 41
confirmation when quitting
  applications, 13–15
connecting to data sources, 6–12
Const keyword, 34
constants in VB 2005, 34–36
constructors, 72
Content control, 145
Content pages, deriving from Master
  Pages, 144–147
ContentPlaceHolder control, 143
Continue keyword, using with loops, 48
ContinueDestinationPageUrl property
  (Login control), 160
controlling implementation of
  classes, 89–97
converting types, 39
Count property, 73
CreateUserWizard control, 157–159
CType function, 77
customizing classes, 66–81

D

data binding, automatic, 6–12
Data Source Configuration Wizard, 105

Data Sources window, 6, 9, 105–108,
  122
data types, 29–31
 aggregating, using structures, 87–88
 converting from one to another, 39
databases
 adding to Windows
  applications, 102–104
 binding data to forms, 105–110,
  122–124
 connecting to, 6–12
DataGridView control, 122–124
 vs. GridView control, 163
DataTips feature, 20
Date type, 30
debug time, inspecting objects
  during, 20
debugging applications, 18
debugging support, improved in
  ASP.NET 2.0, 154
Decimal type, 30
decision-making statements, 43–46
declaring
 arrays, 38
 multiple variables in single
  statement, 33
default constructors, 72
default values for optional
  parameters, 51
defaultValue attribute (profile
  property), 151
defining classes, 82–85
deploying Windows
  applications, 125–129
dereferencing objects, 93
derived classes, 67
_Description private variable, 74
Description property, 73
Design view for web forms, 142
designing classes, 81–88
Dialog windows, adding to projects, 13
Dialog1 control, properties of, 14
DialogResult property, 15
Dim (dimension) keyword, 31
 using within a class, 75
DisplayError method, 118
Dispose method, 94
DivideByZeroException exception, 52
DllImport attribute, 96

DLLs (dynamically linked libraries), commonly referenced, 62
Double type, 30
Do-Until loops, 46
Do-While loops, 46
   exiting from, 48

E

early binding of variables, 31
E-Commerce web service (ECS), 111
edit-and-continue feature, 19
ElseIf keyword, 45
empty constructors, 72
End If statements, 45
enumerations in VB 2005, 35
Equals method, 66
error handling in VB 2005, 51–54
Error List window, 97
event handlers for exiting/closing applications, 15
Exception exception, 52
exceptions, throwing, 53
Exit dialog box
   creating, 13–15
   linking events with, 15
Exit For/Exit Do/Exit While statements, 48
exiting loops, 48
explicit conversions, 40
Explorer Form templates, 20

F

FCL (.NET Framework Class Library), 60–62
File System option for web development, 139
files, managing, using My namespace, 56
Filesystem object (My.Computer), 56
Finalize method, 93
FindControl method, 163
FixIts (issues raised in Code Advisor), 182
folders
   members-only, adding to web applications, 160
   refreshing, 141
For loops, 46
   exiting from, 48

For-Each loops, 46
FormClosing event, 16
forms
   adding menus/toolbars to, 2–6
   binding data to, 105–110, 122–124
   creating, 2
Forms authentication
   default settings for, 167
   vs. Windows authentication, 150
Friend access modifier, 85–87
functions
   invoking, 48
   passing values to, 49–51

G

generic classes, 77
   advantages of, 79
Get accessors, cannot be used with WriteOnly keyword, 74
Get Info button, 113, 131
GetBookInformation method, 114, 132
GetProfile method, 162
GetType operator, 42
GetUser method (Membership class), 153
Global.asax file, 161
GridView control, 163, 167
GripStyle property (MenuStrip control), 27
grouping statements into single line, 44
GUID (Globally Unique Identifier) and anonymous user IDs, 157

H

handling exit/close events, 15
heaps, storing variables in, 31
Help Topics (MSDN), 60
highlighting code edits, 17
HTTP and web services, 113

I

IDisposable interface, 94
If-Then-Else construct, 43–45
IIS, installing on computers, 126
ImageButton control, 152
ImageUrl property, 146
imgBtn_Click method, 151
imgHeader control, 143, 163

imgLogo control, 143
implementation of classes,
        controlling, 89–97
Implements keyword, 92
implicit conversions, 40
Imports keyword, 61
inheritance, 58, 67
Inherits keyword, 67
initializing
    arrays, 38
    using constructors, 72
    variables in same statement, 33
inspecting objects at runtime, 20
instantiating classes, 63
Integer type, 30
IntelliSense feature, 18
    My namespace, 28
interfaces vs. abstract classes, 92
internationalizing web applications,
        improved in ASP.NET
        2.0, 137
intrinsic data types, 30
InvalidCastException exception, 52
Is operator, 66
Is/IsNot operators, 41
IsSynchronized property, 73
itemType structure, 149
iteration statements, 46

L

Label control, 10
    populating dialog windows with, 13
launching Windows applications, 129
lblISBN control, 110
Liberty, Jesse, 78, 97
Like operator, 41
LinkButton control, 160
ListBox control, 113, 120, 134
literals in VB 2005, 35
localization, improved support for, in
        ASP.NET 2.0, 137
logical/bitwise operators, 42
Login control, 159
Login Form templates, 20
login pages
    creating, 158–160
    default settings for, 167
Login.aspx file, 167
LoginName control, 159

LoginStatus control, 159
LoginView control, 159
LogoPictureBox control, 21
Long type, 30
looping statements, 46
loops, exiting or skipping, 48
Lowy, Juval, 97
lstBooks control, 110

M

machine.config.default file, 167
Main.aspx file, 144
Master Pages, 137
    building site templates
        with, 140–143
    checkout pages, creating, 163
    choosing, 144
    editing content of, 145
    login pages, creating, 158
    modifying at runtime, 164
    registration pages, creating, 157
Master property, 163
Membership class, 153
    login forms and, 158
members-only folders, adding to web
        applications, 160
memory
    reclaiming, with Using...End Using
        construct, 95
    representations of value
        types/reference types in, 32
menus, adding to forms, 2–6
MenuStrip control, 4
    adding to forms, 100
    saving location of, 26
methods, 59
    adding new, 70–71
    customizing, 68
    hiding, using Shadows keyword, 71
    overloading, 69
    overridable, allowing or
        preventing, 89
    shared methods, 66
    specifying implementation details
        with, 90–92
Microsoft.VisualBasic namespace, 54
migrating (modernization option), 172
    checklist for choosing, 173
Mod (modulus) operator, 41

modernization options for VB
        applications, 171–173
MSDN Help Topics, 60
MsgBoxResult.Yes constant, 188
MsgBoxStyle.YesNo constant, 188
multithreading, 131
MustInherit keyword, 91
MustOverride keyword, 91
My namespace, 28
    examples of using, 55
    managing files with, 56
    objects exposed by, 54
My.Application object, 54
My.Computer object, 55
My.Forms object, 55
My.Settings object, 55
My.User object, 55
My.WebServices object, 55

N

namespaces, 60
narrowing conversions, 40
nesting If-Then-Else statements, 44
.NET Framework Class Library, 60–62
Network object (My.Computer), 56
Not operator, 42

O

Object type, 30
object-oriented programming (OOP) in
        VB 2005, 58–97
objects, 59
    comparing, 65
    creating, 62–65
    dereferencing, 93
    initializing values in, using
            constructors, 72
    inspecting at runtime, 20
    tagging with attributes, 95–97
    unmanaged, 93
Of keyword, 78
OK_Button control, property of, 15
operators in VB 2005, 41
Option Explicit Off statement, 32
Option Strict On statement, 31, 36, 40
optional arguments, 51
Or operator, 42
OrElse operator, 42, 45
overloading methods, 69

Overloads keyword, 70
Overridable keyword, 89, 90
Overrides keyword, 68, 91
overriding methods, 68
    vs. overloading, 70

P

Page Framework, 137
parent classes, 67
Partial classes, 78–81
Partial keyword prefix, 80
passing values to
        subroutines/functions, 49–51
picCover control, 110
PictureBox control, 107
PlaySystemSound method, 118
Pop method, 64
    overriding, 89
pop/push operations, 63
PostBackUrl property
    Checkout button, 165
    LinkButton control, 160
PrintMessage subroutine, 49
Private access modifier, 75, 85–87
Profile objects vs. Session objects, 147
profile property, 150
    attributes in, 151
Profile_MigrateAnonymous event
        handler, 162
ProfileMigrateEventArgs class, 162
profiles of users, migrating from
        anonymous to
        authenticated, 161–165
Programming .NET Components, 97
Programming Visual Basic 2005, 78, 97
projects
    adding Dialog windows to, 13
    creating, 2
properties, 59
    adding to classes, 73–75
    read-only and write-only, 74
    setting for controls, 14–15
Property keyword, 73
PropertyBinding property (ToolStrip
        control), 25
Protected access modifier, 85–87
provider attribute (profile
        property), 151
Public access modifier, 85–87

publishing Windows
applications, 125–129
Push method
overloading, 69
overriding, 68, 89

Q

quitting applications, 13–15

R

RCWs (Runtime Callable
Wrappers), 176
readOnly attribute (profile
property), 151
ReadOnly keyword, 74
reallocating controls, 110
records, browsing, 6–12
redundant conditions, reducing
checking of, 45
reference types, 31
assigning value of one to another, 33
refreshing folders, 141
RegFree COM (Registration-Free
COM), 179
Register.aspx page, 166
registration pages, creating, 157
replacing (modernization option), 173
checklist for choosing, 174
republishing Windows
applications, 134
resizing controls, 110
resources, unnecessary, disposing of, 95
restricting unauthorized access to
pages, 160
Return keyword, 49
reusing classes, 67
reusing (modernization option), 173
checklist for choosing, 174
rewriting (modernization option), 173
checklist for choosing, 174
running applications, 18
Runtime Callable Wrappers
(RCWs), 176
runtime errors, 51
handling, with Try-Catch-Finally
statements, 52
RunWorkerAsync method, 132
RunWorkerCompleted event, 134

S

saving state of applications, 24–27
SByte type, 30
scope of variables, 32
search results, displaying, 116–118
Search Results window, 114, 120
Select-Case construct, 46
SelectedIndexChanged event, 117
serializeAs attribute (profile
property), 151
Set accessors, cannot be used with
ReadOnly keyword, 74
Shadows keyword, 71
shared methods, 66
shopping carts, creating, 147–157
Short type, 30
short-circuiting technique, 45
ShowDialog method, 23
sideline coloring, 17
signatures of methods, 69
Single type, 30
site templates, building using Master
Pages, 140–143
SizeMode property
LogoPictureBox control, 22
picCover control, 110
skipping loops, 48
smart clients, 125
Smart Tasks menu, displaying, 5
snaplines, 14
SOAP (Simple Object Access Protocol)
and web services, 113
Solution Explorer
Content pages, creating, 144
creating About box forms, 21
Master Pages, creating, 140
shopping carts, creating, 148
start pages and, 154
using Upgrade Wizard, 186
sounds, playing different types of, 118
Source view for web forms, 142
Splash Screen templates, 20
SplitContainer control, 102
SQL Server 2005 Express
downloading, 7
Stack class (System.Collections), 63
stacks, 63
storing variables in, 31

statements, 43–47
  grouping into single lines using :
    (colon), 44
static methods, 66
StatusLabel control, 101, 112
StatusStrip control
  accessing web services, 112
  adding to forms, 101
stepping through code, 19
String type, 30
StringBuilder class, 37
strings in VB 2005, 37
strong passwords, 166
strongly typed variables, 31
  vs. weakly typed variables, 76
Structure keyword, 87–88
structured error handling, 52
structures vs. classes, 88
Sub Finalize procedure, 93
Sub New procedure, 72
subroutines
  invoking, 49
  passing values to, 49–51
symbolic constants, 35
SyncRoot property, 73
syntax of VB 2005 language, 29–57
System namespace, 61
System.Collections namespace, 61
System.Collections.Generic
  namespace, 78
System.ComponentModel
  namespace, 132
System.Data namespace, 61
System.Web.UI namespace, 61
System.Windows.Forms namespace, 61

T

tables
  choosing which ones to work
    with, 105
  creating, 104
  making accessible to users, 10
  navigating through, 10
templates, new, in VB 2005, 20
testing
  web applications, 166–167
  Windows applications, 120, 124
Text property, 14
Themes and Skins, 137

threading, 130
Throw keyword, 53
TitlesTableAdapter control, 119
toolbars, adding to forms, 2–6
ToolStrip control, 4
  adding to forms, 100
  coding exit event of, 16
  saving location of, 25–27
ToolStripContainer control, 4
  BindingNavigator control and, 11
ToolStripLocation setting, 26
Track Changes option and sideline
  coloring, 17
Try...Catch...Finally statements, 52
txtAuthors control, 110
txtKeywords control, 110
txtPrice control, 110
txtPublisher control, 110
txtTitle control, 110
type characters in VB 2005, 34
type conversion, 39
types, data (see data types)

U

UInteger type, 30, 33
ULong type, 30, 33
unauthorized access to pages,
  restricting, 160
unmanaged objects, 93
unsigned data type support in VB
  2005, 33
unstructured error handling, 52
Upgrade Wizard, 185–188
_UpgradeReport.htm document, 186
upgrading VB 6 applications
  making the right decision, 173–175
  using Code Advisor for Visual Basic
    6.0, 180–185
  using Upgrade Wizard, 185–188
user accounts, creating, 157
user-defined types (UDT), 30
users
  authenticating with My.User, 56
  restricting unauthorized access to
    pages, 160
  transferring anonymous profile info
    to user profiles, 161–165
  validating credentials for, using
    Membership class, 153

UShort type, 30, 33
Using...End Using construct, 95

V

value types, 30
   assigning value of one to another, 32
variables, 31–34
   access modifiers and, 85–87
   multiple, declaring in single
      statement, 33
   weakly typed vs. strongly typed, 76
Variant type, 29
VB 2005
   moving to, from VB 6, 171–188
   using legacy COM objects
      in, 176–179
VB 6
   changes made to the language, 60
   moving from, to VB 2005, 171–188
   upgrading applications
      using Code Advisor for Visual
        Basic 6.0, 180–185
      using Upgrade Wizard, 185–188

W

weakly typed vs. strongly typed
      variables, 76
web applications, 136–170
   commonly referenced DLLs, 62
   creating, 138–147
   login pages, creating, 158–160
   registration pages, creating, 157
   testing, 166–167
web references, adding to
      Amazon.com, 111
web services, 113
   accessing Amazon.com, 112–116
   accessing asynchronously, 130–134
   My.WebServices object and, 56

web services calls and
      multithreading, 131
Web.config file, 153
Web.config files, adding to
      projects, 149
<WebMethod( )> attribute, 95
While loops, 46
   exiting from, 48
whitespace in VB 2005 language, 43
widening conversions, 40
Windows applications, 98–135
   adding databases to
      projects, 102–104
   automatically updating, 130–135
   binding data to forms, 105–110,
      122–124
   building the main window, 100–102
   commonly referenced DLLs, 62
   creating, 2, 99
   deploying, 125–129
   republishing, 134
   saving information to databases, 118
   search results, displaying, 116–118
   testing, 120, 124
   viewing information
      offline, 121–125
Windows vs. Forms authentication, 150
With...End With construct, 75
WriteOnly keyword, 74
WSDL (Web Services Description
      Language) and web
      services, 113

X

XML and web services, 113
XmlInclude attribute, 149
Xor operator, 42

About the Author

Wei-Meng Lee (Microsoft MVP) is a technologist and founder of Developer Learning Solutions (*http://www.developerlearningsolutions.com*), a technology company specializing in hands-on training in the latest Microsoft technologies. Wei-Meng speaks regularly at international conferences and has authored numerous books on .NET, XML, and wireless technologies, including *ASP.NET 2.0: A Developer's Notebook* and the *.NET Compact Framework Pocket Guide* (both from O'Reilly). He writes extensively for the O'Reilly Network on topics ranging from .NET to Mac OS X. Wei-Meng is currently a Microsoft Regional Director for Singapore. Visit Wei-Meng's blog at *http://weimenglee.blogspot.com*.

Colophon

Our look is the result of reader comments, our own experimentation, and feedback from distribution channels. Distinctive covers complement our distinctive approach to technical topics, breathing personality and life into potentially dry subjects.

The animals on the cover of *Visual Basic 2005 Jumpstart* are moor frogs (*Rana arvalis*). The moor frog is one of only six frog species found in Europe and one of only three found north of the Arctic Circle. Despite their broad distribution, which extends from central Europe to northern Balkan and even up to the Ural Mountains in Russia, they are one of the rarest frogs in Europe.

Moor frogs thrive in bogs, alder marshlands, and inshore waters. They hibernate at the bottom of pools or on dry land in rotten woodpiles or in piles of rotting leaves. In early spring, once the ice and frost have melted, they reappear for the mating season. Mating takes places in the water, with eager males assembling in anticipation before the females arrive. During the height of the breeding period, males turn bright blue because of the high concentration of lymph underneath their skin. The incessant mating call—which has been compared to the sound of air escaping from an empty, submerged bottle—reveals the male's excitement.

The bright blue skin, characteristic of the mating season, is a marked difference from their usual appearance; color and patterns vary greatly from uniform brown to black blotches. Although moor frogs bear a strong resemblance to common frogs, they often have a pale vertebral stripe running from the snout to the cloaca that helps to distinguish them. Also, male and female moor frogs average in size between 4–8 cm, while common frogs average 10 cm.

Earthworms, flies, beetles, butterflies, and ants are among some of the species that comprise the moor frog's diet. They also have been known to dine on snails—swallowing them whole or cracking the shell in their mouths. Some of the predators they have to worry about include cyprinid fish, grass snakes, storks, fox, and hedges. If a moor frog feels threatened while on dry land, he will first make a long, high jump, and then burrow in soil or beneath a clump of grass.

Adam Witwer was the production editor and Linley Dolby was the copyeditor for *Visual Basic 2005 Jumpstart*. Jeffrey Liggett proofread the text. Abby Fox, Genevieve d'Entremont, and Claire Cloutier provided quality control. Judy Hoer wrote the index.

Ellie Volckhausen designed the cover of this book, based on a series design by Edie Freedman. The cover image is from the Library of Natural History. Karen Montgomery produced the cover layout with Adobe InDesign CS using Adobe's ITC Garamond font.

David Futato designed the interior layout. This book was converted by Keith Fahlgren to FrameMaker 5.5.6 with a format conversion tool created by Erik Ray, Jason McIntosh, Neil Walls, and Mike Sierra that uses Perl and XML technologies. The text font is Linotype Birka; the heading font is Adobe Myriad Condensed; and the code font is LucasFont's TheSans Mono Condensed. The illustrations that appear in the book were produced by Robert Romano, Jessamyn Read, and Lesley Borash using Macromedia FreeHand MX and Adobe Photoshop CS. The tip and warning icons were drawn by Christopher Bing. This colophon was written by Loranah Dimant.

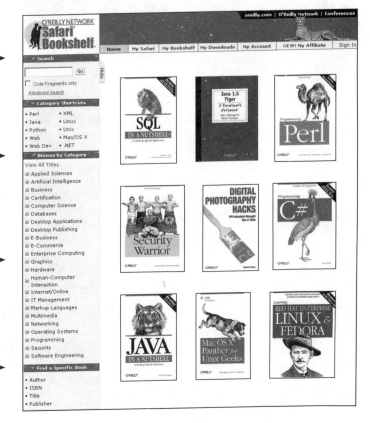

Related Titles from O'Reilly

Visual Basic 2005: A Developer's Notebook

By Matthew MacDonald
April 2005,
ISBN 0-596-00726-4
262 pages,
$29.95 US, $41.95 CA

To bring you up to speed with Visual Basic 2005, this practical book offers nearly 50 hands-on projects. Each one explores a new feature of the language, with emphasis on changes that can increase productivity, simplify programming tasks, and help you add new functionality to your applications. You get the goods straight from the masters in an informal, code-intensive style. Part of our new Developer's Notebook series.

ASP.NET 2.0: A Developer's Notebook

By Wei-Meng Lee
June 2005,
ISBN 0-596-00812-0
348 pages,
$29.95 US, $41.95 CA

To bring you up to speed with ASP.NET 2.0, this practical book offers nearly 50 hands-on projects. Each one explores a new feature of the language, with emphasis on changes that can increase productivity, simplify programming tasks, and help you add new functionality to your applications. You get the goods straight from the masters in an informal, code-intensive style. Part of our new Developer's Notebook series.

Programming Visual Basic 2005

By Jesse Liberty
September 2005,
ISBN 0-596-00949-6
576 pages,
$39.95 US, $55.95 CA

This information-packed guide helps you understand Visual Basic 2005, the next-generation release of the popular Visual Basic programming language. This book aims to make you immediately productive in creating Windows and web applications using Visual Basic 2005 and all of its tools. Perfect for experienced VB6 and VB.NET developers.

Programming .NET Components

By Juval Löwy
July 2005,
ISBN 0-596-10207-0
644 pages,
$44.95 US, $62.95 CA

Programming .NET Components, Second Edition is the consummate introduction to the Microsoft .NET Framework—the technology of choice for building components on Windows platforms. From its many lessons, tips, and guidelines, readers will learn how to use the .NET Framework to program reusable, maintainable, and robust components. Following in the footsteps of its best-selling predecessor, Programming .NET Components, Second Edition has been updated to cover .NET 2.0.